Preface

Wireless networks are based on radio communications and operate within the 2.4-2.4853 GHz range of the ISM radio band, and are standardised by IEEE 802.11. Although they have major advantages they also have a number of security issues. Signal leakage means that network communications can be picked up outside the physical boundaries of the building in which they are being operated, meaning a hacker can operate from the street outside or discretely from blocks away. In addition to signal leakage wireless networks have various other weaknesses. Wired Equivalent Privacy (WEP), the protocol used within Wireless LAN's (WLAN's) to provide the equivalent security of wired networks is inherently weak. The use of the RC4 algorithm and weak IV's makes WEP a vulnerable security measure. In addition to WEP's weaknesses there are various other attacks that can be initiated against WLAN's, all with detrimental effects.

The book closes with recommendations for three groups of user. These are home users, Small Office/Home Office (SOHO) and medium to large organisations. Home users should implement all the security measures their hardware offers them, to include WEP at the longest key length permitted. The home office section of the SOHO group should utilise all the built-in security measures and implement firewalls on all connected PCs and change their WEP key on a weekly basis. The Small Office section of the SOHO group should implement WPA-SPK; and the Medium to Large Organisations should implement one or more of either WPA Enterprise with a RADIUS server, VPN software, IDSs, and provide documented policies in relation to WLANs and their use.

This book aims to introduce the area of wireless (Wi-Fi, 802.11) security with particular emphasis on WEP. Weaknesses are highlighted through the art of war-driving where unprotected access points are discovered. War driving used ethically can be a powerful tool in the hands of security professionals to test the security of the networks they are charged with protecting.

TABLE OF CONTENTS

LIST OF FIGURES IN MAIN TEXT

LIST OF TABLES IN MAIN TEXT

1   Introduction

Networks, acting as the veins through which data flows, have advanced. Traditionally networks consisted of various devices that were connected together solely by cabling, however, there is now an alternative. This alternative takes cabling (and its associated issues) away and replaces it with a more flexible and cost effective method for the transmission of data. It's a technology that has been in use for many years, but is only now being realised within the networking world particularly in the implementation of Local Area Networks (LANs). The migration to this new style of networking, although slow at the start, has taken off in an almost explosive manner in recent years. This relatively new networking medium is radio communications.

Traditionally LANs were implemented using cables, with each device being attached to the network by means of a Network Interface Card (NIC), cable and connectors. The idea behind the cable was to provide a means through which data could travel in the form of discrete electrical signals. The data would propagate along the cable (usually copper wire) by conduction, and as long as there was a circuit the data would propagate. In this model the data is enclosed within and travels between devices, through connectors and along cables. As such, this enclosure provides some level of protection for data by encasing it within wire, shielding and plastic.

A typical configuration in a small organisation may consist of a number of desk-top and/or laptop Personal Computers (PCs), printers and perhaps a server, all with NICs, cabling and either a switch or hub, a patch-panel, and possibly a router to connect them to the Internet and the outside world. The PC's NIC would be connected to a face-plate by a short cable, the face-plate would normally be installed on the wall behind or beside the PC; the cabling behind the face-plate would then run back to a patch-panel, which would then be linked to a switch or hub via patch leads, and then everything would perhaps connect to a router.

This type of configuration works extremely well, however, the initial cabling costs can be high depending on the cable used. In addition, some buildings can be difficult to wire, especially older ones. Another important disadvantage is that wired networks can be somewhat inflexible. Should the structure of the organisation change and PCs need to be moved or additional PCs need to be added to the network, cabling can become an issue.

It also limits the mobility of users, possibly prohibiting them from bringing their PCs into meetings or using them in another location in the building that doesn't have wired network access. However, these issues can be overcome through the use of wireless devices and connections. As well as the flexibility offered by Wireless Local Area Networks (WLANs), they can also help significantly boost productivity. A survey, carried out in 2003 on 400 American medium and large sized organisations, found that WLANs gave end users the ability to be connected to the network, on average, 3.5 more hours per day. This, the research claims, makes staff up to a third more productive than they would had they been connected to a wired network (Jaques, 2003).

In their White Paper, 'Deploying 802.11 Wireless LANs', 3Com provide a number of advantages for organisations implementing WLANs, these are outlined below:

➲ **Productivity Increases**
As mentioned above, because employees are connected for longer, productivity will obviously increase. WLANs provide coverage in areas where network connections were not available or possible before, meaning employees are able to access the Internet, e-mail and network files, independent of where they are in the building. Time between meetings can be utilised for productivity gains and immediate access to critical information can also provide huge benefits.

➲ **Improved Efficiency at Meetings**
Information can be shared effortlessly at meetings, even with people who are not employees.

Members, who are authorised, can access pertinent corporate information in real time and relay data to help speed decision making processes. Visitors can be effortlessly set up with limited access to certain information and services whilst on site and become actively involved in the meeting with no cabling issues to overcome.

➲ **Ease of New Installations**
WLANs dramatically reduce the time and cost of adding PCs and laptops to an established network. A complete WLAN could be set-up within a few hours, as opposed to a few days or weeks for a wired equivalent. There's no need to create cut-sheets, drill holes, pull cables from the wiring closet all around the building, simply plug in a wireless Access Point (AP), configure a few basic settings, and users with wireless NICs are ready to connect.

➲ **Off-Site Connectivity**
A laptop or PDA with WLAN capabilities, i.e. with a wireless card installed, allow mobile users to be more productive when they are travelling by using public 'hot spots' at airports, hotels and coffee bars, to access e-mails and even the corporate network enabling them to make use of all those wasted hours sitting at the airport waiting on a delayed flight.

➲ **Temporary Networks**
Temporary networks can be achieved with minimal effort at off-site training-sessions, trade-shows and meetings. All the equipment can be carried to the site and set-up with minimum effort. Any visitors wishing to join, perhaps to download or copy company/product information, can be connected in a matter of minutes and then easily disconnected again.

➲ **Reduced Installation Costs**
The cost of running cables can vary, especially in environments where it is difficult to lay wires;

inevitably this will drive the cost of networking upwards. Wireless connections eliminate the issue of cabling completely, and significantly ease the implementation of networks, thus lowering costs. For inter-building connections, wireless point-to-point bridges are ideal; the cost of renting expensive T1/E1 links is no longer an issue; they can be replaced with various wireless bridges (one on each building).

⊃   **Enhanced Flexibility**
Probably the most advantageous aspect of WLANs is their flexibility. Users aren't tied to their desks by cables and wires, they are free to roam throughout the company and take their PC with them. As long as they're within the range of the network, they can take their work to the car park, if so desired. Network administrators can add flexibility to their networking plans, WLANs allow them to do things that may have otherwise been unfeasible to do due to the limitations of cabling. (3Com Corporation, 2003)

A WLAN can be easily integrated into an existing wired LAN to provide an extended, wired/wireless hybrid LAN. To the user the operation of the network would appear un-changed, however they will be able to enjoy the many advantages that WLANs have to offer.

The next chapter provides a background of how wireless technology works. How it is applied within LANs will be examined, followed by a discussion of its unique security vulnerabilities and the security solutions available for WLANs, leading up to the methodology, research and findings. The book concludes with various recommendations targeting three categories of wireless users; the home user, Small Office/Home Office (SOHO) and medium to large organisations.

2   Wireless Security

The purpose of this chapter is to provide an overview of the technologies utilized within Wireless Local Area Networks (WLANs). It is important to understand the technologies upon which WLANs are based before an appreciation of their inherent weaknesses can occur.

2.1 Basic Radio Communications

On the surface WLANs function the same as their wired counterparts, transporting data between network devices. However, there is one fundamental, and quite significant, difference; WLANs are based upon radio communications technology, as an alternative to structured wiring and cables. Data is transmitted between devices through the air by utilizing the radio waves. Devices that participate in a WLAN must have a Network Interface Card (NIC) with wireless capabilities. This essentially means that the card contains a small radio device that allows it to communicate with other wireless devices, within the defined range for that card, for example, the 2.4-2.4853 GHz range.   For a device to participate in a wireless network it must, firstly, be permitted to communicate with the devices in that network and, secondly, it must be within the transmission range of the devices in that network.

To communicate, radio-based devices take advantage of electromagnetic waves and their ability to be altered in such a manner that they can carry information, known as modulation.   Information is transferred by mixing the electromagnetic wave with the information to be transmitted. At the receiving end, the signal is compared to an un-modulated signal to reverse the process (called demodulation).

There are basically three main types of modulation techniques; these are Amplitude Modulation (AM), Frequency Modulation (FM), and Phase Modulation (PM). Because FM is more robust against interference, it was chosen as the modulation standard for high frequency

9

radio transmissions. See Appendix I for a brief overview of these modulation techniques (Harte, et al, 2000). Radio devices utilized within WLANs operate in the 2.4-2.4845GHz range of the unlicensed Industrial Scientific and Medical (ISM) frequency band, using either Frequency Hopping Spread Spectrum (FHSS) or Direct Sequence Spread Spectrum (DSSS), which are special modulation techniques used for spreading data over a wide band of frequencies sacrificing bandwidth to gain signal-to-noise (S/N) performance. See Appendix II for information on both of these techniques (Harte et al, 2000).

2.2 Wireless Network Components

A basic WLAN configuration may include some or all the following components:

- wireless access point (for infrastructure mode);
- mobile devices;
- fixed devices; and
- wireless Network Interface Cards (NICs).

A WLAN provides connectivity over the airwaves within a local area, such as a building.

Wireless Access Point (AP). An AP is a piece of hardware that connects wireless clients to a wired network. It usually has at least two network connections and the wireless interface is typically an onboard radio or an embedded PCMCIA[1] wireless card. The second network interface can be Ethernet, a dial-up modem or even another wireless adapter. The AP hardware controls access to and from both networks. It can also offer other services to the network, such as Dynamic Host Configuration Protocol (DHCP)[2] and Network Address Translation (NAT)[3] (Flickenger, 2002).

Mobile Devices. This includes laptops, Personal Digital Assistants (PDAs), tablet PCs and other similar devices, that workers can carry with them. However, they will not be able to access the WLAN unless the devices are fitted with a wireless NIC and are properly configured. Today more and more devices are being released to market with

---

[1] Personal Computer Memory Card International Association. An industry group organized in 1989 to promote standards for a credit card-sized memory input-output device that would fit all PCs. (Webopedia)
[2] DHCP is a protocol that provides a means of dynamically allocating IP address to computers on a LAN. (FOLFOC)
[3] NAT, an internet standard, will allow the AP to support multiple wireless users while only requiring a single IP address for the wire. Traffic for a device on the LAN is addressed to the AP who then forwards the packet to the appropriate device. (Whatis.com)

wireless capabilities pre-installed, like Intel's new Centrino[4] range, launched in March 2003.

Fixed Devices. This includes desktop PCs, file servers and larger printers which can be fitted with wireless NICs. These devices have wireless capabilities because of where they are located in a building, perhaps in a room with no wired network connections, or perhaps to extend an existing network or provide extra services without the need to cable.

Wireless Network Interface Cards (NICs). These are key to allowing WLAN participation. Devices can come with them pre-installed, but at the moment the most prevalent type of wireless NIC is the PCMCIA for laptops, and the internal PCI card which slots into an unused communications port on the back of a desktop PC. Each NIC has a unique Media Access Control (MAC) address burned into it at manufacture, to uniquely identify it; it also contains a small radio device and an antenna. However, the NIC must be compatible with the AP before communication can occur. For example, an 802.11b card needs an 802.11b[5] AP.

---

[4] The Centrino range integrates wireless capabilities into a new generation of mobile PCs, with a new mobile processor, related chipsets and 802.11 wireless network functions, and extended battery life, and thinner and lighter notebook designs.
http://www.intel.com/pressroom/archive/releases/20030312comp.htm
[5] 802.11 is the IEEE standard which governs wireless network communications, the 'b' denotes the amendment to the original standard. 802.11b governs devices operating in the 2.4-2.4853GHz range at 11Mpbs. (IEEE)

2.3 WLAN Network Modes

Wireless devices have the option of participating in two type of networks; Ad Hoc and Infrastructure. An Ad Hoc (also known as peer-to-peer) network is the simplest form of WLAN. It is composed of two or more nodes communicating without any bridging or forwarding capability; all nodes are of equal importance and may join and leave the network at any time, each device also has equal right to the medium. Access Points (APs) are not necessary. Figure 1 below demonstrates this.

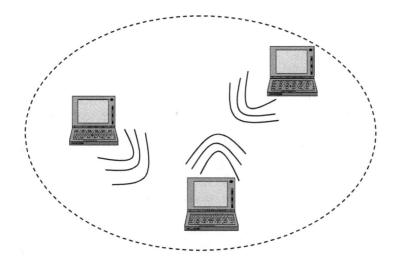

Figure 1: Ad-Hoc Network Topology

For this to work, the devices wishing to participate in an Ad Hoc network must be within transmission range of each other, when a nodes goes out of range it will lose connection with the rest of the devices. The range of this type of network is referred to as a 'single cell' and is called an Independent Basic Service Set (IBSS) (Tourrilhes, 2000).

In an infrastructure network communications take place through an AP, in a many-to-one configuration, with the AP at the single end. In its simplest form it consists of one AP and a group of wireless clients/devices, which must be within transmission range of the AP, and be properly configured to communicate with the AP. This type of network is called a Basic Service Set (BSS). (Sikora, 2003)

If two or more BSSes are operated in the same network, by linking the APs via a background network, this is then called an Extended Service Set (ESS). Such a configuration can cover larger, multi-floor, buildings. However, support is required for 'roaming' between different APs on the network, that is the hand-off between a device leaving one APs range and going into the range of another AP (Geier, 1999).

APs can be overlapped if they are each given a different channel, within the 2.4-2.4835GHz, range to communicate on. There are eleven overlapping frequencies specified in IEEE 802.11, which means that with careful planning multiple networks can coexist in the same physical space without interfering with each other (Tourrilhes, 2000). APs must also be configured with a Service Set Identifier (SSID), also known as the network name. It is a simple 1-32 byte alphanumeric string given to each ESS that identifies the wireless network and allows stations to connect to one desired network when multiple independent networks operate in the same physical area. It also provides a very basic way of preventing unauthorised users from joining your network, as all devices in an ESS must have the same ESSID to participate.

Most APs can provide additional, basic, security features, such as WEP and MAC address filtering. WEP, an abbreviation for Wired Equivalent Protocol, is a protocol designed specifically for use on wireless networks and is supposed to provide the security equivalent of the cable in a wired network through the use of encryption. Communicating devices must use the same WEP key in order to communicate. MAC address filtering provides a basis for screening users wanting to connect to a network; for a client device to be able to successfully communicate with the AP, its name must appear on an access control list of MAC addresses held by that AP.

However, both these methods have been proven weak in their ability to secure wireless networks; both can be easily penetrated.

2.4 WLAN Market Growth

The growth of the wireless industry has been explosive in recent years, mostly attributed to the keen adoption of 802.11b equipment, the cost of which continues to decrease annually, making them a more affordable option. They offer various advantages to users and network administrators alike. According to Forrester, there will be 53 million Wi-Fi enabled laptops and PDAs in Europe by 2008. With wireless access set to be introduced into pubs and clubs in addition to railway stations, hotels, coffee shops and other public places, possibly even trains, it can only get bigger. (Broersma, 2003)

IDC predicts that the worldwide market for wireless LAN devices will grow to £3 billion in 2006, from £485 million in 2000. The number of wireless NICs and APs shipped over that time is expected to reach 11.8 million units, from 2.8 million in 2000. There is no doubt the WLAN market is booming, the use of WLANs is surging. (Rysavy, 2001 and Intel IT e-business Group, 2004)

Indeed, figures just in for the year 2003 strengthens the trend. Worldwide Wi-Fi hardware shipments more than tripled in 2003 to £14.3 million network NICs and APs, up from £5.2 million in 2002. According to research from Instat/MDR, projections for 2006 indicate sales will reach a staggering £25 million. (The 802.11 Report, 2004)

Traditionally, WLANs have seen greatest acceptance in industrial markets, such as healthcare, inventory control and warehousing, where companies could justify high equipment and integration costs because the applications provide a clear return on investment. However, within the last few years, use has expanded into commercial markets, including mainstream businesses, homes and educational environments.

However, this widespread adoption has magnified the security flaws inherent in wireless technologies. WLANs are extremely useful, but the encryption and authentication methods specified in the 802.11 standard are flawed, causing serious security issues.

2.5 Standards

IEEE 802.11 basically identifies an 'over-the-air' interface between two, or more, wireless devices. The Wireless Local Area Networks Standards Working group was formed in 1990, with the task of forming a global standard for radio equipment and networks. 802.11 essentially builds upon 802.3, adding wireless-networking protocols. There are three main IEEE standards which govern wireless communications in LANs; these are 802.11b, 802.11a and 802.11g. There are numerous extensions to these standards, and indeed one can become rather confused at the sheer number of letters that can be put after 802.11. For a comprehensive overview of all the 802.11 standards please refer to Appendix III.

2.6 Tools used for WLAN Security Probing

One common tool for probing wireless networks is Netstumbler for Windows. This software is readily available online and is relatively easy to set up and use. Another common software package is Ethereal. This software enables the gathering and analysis of the contents of network transmissions. These can be run on a Windows laptop with a 802.11x PCMCIA card and an external antenna (e.g. Maxima 5dB antenna with a magnetic base). Sometimes you can pick both an antenna and NetStumbler kit up together. This is known as the 'NetStumbler Kit'.

A 5dB omnidirectional antenna is roof mountable with a magnetic base, and has an estimated range of half a mile. it is also more inconspicuous than larger antenna due to its small size (around 6 inches tall including the base). An omnidirectional antenna should be chosen because of the way it transmits and receives, that is in all directions, as opposed to a single focused direction. This creates better coverage and increases the probability of picking up devices whilst driving.

In addition, as NetStumbler can receive GPS information, a Garmin GPS device can also be utilised to effectively 'map' the locations of discovered WLAN devices. The GPS aspect of NetStumbler's software keeps a real-time log of devices' position by mapping the longitude and latitude coordinates. This information can be easily imported into software called StumbVerter in conjunction with MS's Mappoint, and used to create colourful and accurate maps for identifying WLAN devices and their range.

Figure 2: NetStumbler Screen Shot

Initial scans to identify wireless networks can be carried out using NetStumbler, as it identifies the signal strength, channel and location. When driving it is easy to recognize if a device has been discovered as NetStumbler provides an audio sound, which persists for the duration of the connection. If an active device is within range it will be listed in the main window within the software, with a circle beside the listed device highlighted in green. If the transmission is encrypted, a small lock will appear within the circle, it will also display the type of encryption employed, for example, WEP. Figure 2 shows a screen-shot of NetStumbler's output.

Other information supplied includes the SSID, manufacturer of the device signalling and its MAC address. There are also a number of useful filters that can be applied to quickly sort multiple networks on criteria such as WEP usage or whether the network is an IBSS or BSS type. This is information that can later be used to configure the laptop to join the network or use a shared internet connection. APs and clients send beacons and broadcasts, respectively, to find one another. AP's beacons are sent at predefined intervals, and are essentially invitations and directions that enable a client to find an AP and configure the appropriate settings to communicate. A beacon announces the SSID and the channel that the network is operating on. NetStumbler uses all this information to create its output (Sutton, 2002).

To provide some background, the following chapter will outline the various weaknesses inherent in WLANs and the types of attacks that can be implemented against them. As mentioned earlier, recommendations will be made to three categories of wireless users; home, small office home office (SOHO) and medium to large organisations later in the book. These users will either be currently operating a wireless device or WLAN, or are contemplating implementing them at some in the future.

2.7 Focus of Book

There are various security options available to protect WLAN devices, however, not all users implement them. The primary field research will identify how many devices are actually protected. The aim of this Book is to investigate the current state of WLAN security and demonstrate exploits that can be adopted by rogue hackers. The purpose of demonstrating exploits in this book is so as to provide IT security professionals with the necessary knowledge needed to protect against these exploits.

Due to the nature of this book and the ethical issues it raises, no active attacks will be attempted against any of the devices/networks identified. Alternatively a test WLAN will be used to demonstrate the affect of leaving a network unprotected and the consequences. The attacks instigated against the test WLAN will be real attacks that can also be carried out against live networks.

Further, the test WLAN will be used to evaluate the relative strength of a selection of security options and how these survive a range of attacks. The results from these tests, together with literary research, will be used as a basis for security recommendations to the three groups of users identified earlier.

3 Wired Equivalent Privacy

With the emergence of any new technology there are always the unanticipated problems that occur after release. Because most testing is carried out within a closed environment, or perhaps because not enough testing was carried out, some issues are not realised until a technology makes it into the real world. Unfortunately, this is also true of WLAN technologies, but the implications are not small. It goes to the very core of every network and affects their most vital element - security. Wired networks have always presented their own security issues, but wireless networks introduce a whole new set of rules with their own unique security vulnerabilities. Most wired security measures are just not appropriate for application within a WLAN environment; this is mostly due to the complete change in transmission medium.

However, some of the security implementations developed specifically for WLANs are also not terribly strong. Indeed, this aspect could be viewed as a 'work-in-progress'; new vulnerabilities are being discovered just as quickly as security measures are being released. Perhaps the issue that has received the most publicity is the major weaknesses in WEP, and more particularly the use of the RC4 algorithm and relatively short Initialisation Vectors (IVs).

3.1 Signal Leakage

WLANs suffer from all the security risks associated with their wired counterparts, however, they also introduce some unique risks of their own. The main issue with radio-based wireless networks is signal leakage. Due to the properties of radio transmissions it is impossible to contain signals within one clearly defined area. In addition, because data is not enclosed within cable it makes it very easy to intercept without being physically connected to the network. This puts it outside the limits of what a user can physically control; signals can be received outside the building and even from streets away.

Two Kansas University researchers, Matt Dunbar and Brett Becker, mapped the signals leaking from wireless networks in their local area to highlight just how far they can propagate. See Figure 3 for a view of just how far signal leakage can go.

Figure 3: Signal Leakage from a WLAN

(**Source:** http://www.ittc.ku.edu/wlan/)

Dunbar and Becker took raw data collected from Netstumbler probes and used this, along with their knowledge of modern mapping techniques, to give wireless users a dramatic insight into how WLANs can easily extend beyond their intended range.

The maps they produced show black and white aerial photographs with signal strengths shown in colours ranging from blue to orange; blue indicating very strong signals and orange indicating very weak signals. They were subsequently used as a basis for promoting wireless security awareness, and how it could be improved (Sutherland, 2002).

Signal leakage may not be a huge priority when organisations are implementing their WLAN, but it can present a significant security issue, as demonstrated below. The same signals that are transmitting data around an organisation's office, are the same signals that can also be picked up from streets away by an unknown third party. This is what makes WLANs so vulnerable. Before WLANs became mainstream, someone wishing to gain unauthorised access to a wired network had to physically attach themselves to a cable within the building. This is why wiring closets should be kept locked and secured. Any potential hacker had to take great risks to penetrate a wired network.

Today potential hackers do not have to use extreme measures, there's no need to smuggle equipment on site when it can be done from the car park, or from two streets away. It isn't difficult for someone to obtain the necessary equipment, access can be gained in a very discrete manner from a distance. In fact, some of the equipment can be made at home, with the now infamous Pringles can being proof of this. See Appendix IV for details on the Pringles can antenna.

3.2 Wired Equivalent Protocol (WEP)

To go some way towards providing the same level of security the cable provides in wired networks, the Wired Equivalent Protocol (WEP) was developed. IEEE 802.11 defined three basic security services for the WLAN environment (Karygiannis and Owens):

- Authentication (a primary goal of WEP)
- Confidentiality (privacy – a second goal of WEP)
- Integrity (another goal of WEP)

WEP was designed to provide the security of a wired LAN by encryption through use of the RC4 (Rivest Code 4) algorithm. It's primary function was to safeguard against eavesdropping ('sniffing'), by making the data that is transmitted unreadable by a third party who does not have the correct WEP key to decrypt the data.

RC4 is not specific to WEP, it is a random generator, also known as a keystream generator or a stream cipher, and was developed in RSA Laboratories by Ron Rivest in 1987 (hence the name Rivest Code (RC)). It takes a relatively short input and produces a somewhat longer output, called a pseudo-random key stream. This key stream is simply added modulo two, that is exclusive ORed (XOR), with the data to be transmitted, to generate what is known as ciphertext. See Figure 4.

One can also visit http://www.wisdom.weizmann.ac.il /~itsik/RC4/rc4.html or consult (Tyrrell, 2003) for more detailed examples.

Two (00000010 in binary) is the encrypting variable (key). It is XORed with some plain text to produce ciphertext. For this example we will use the plain text message "HI".

	H	**I**	
	0 1 0 0 1 0 0 0	0 1 0 0 1 0 0 1	←
XOR	0 0 0 0 0 0 1 0	0 0 0 0 0 0 1 0	**Encrypted**
	0 1 0 0 1 0 1 0	0 1 0 0 1 0 1 1	**text**

The recipient has a copy of the same key and uses it to generate an identical key stream. XORing this key stream with the ciphertext results in the original plain text:

	0 1 0 0 1 0 1 0	0 1 0 0 1 0 1 1	←
XOR	0 0 0 0 0 0 1 0	0 0 0 0 0 0 1 0	**Encrypted**
	0 1 0 0 1 0 0 0	0 1 0 0 1 0 0 1	**text**
	H	**I**	

Figure 4: Ciphertext Example

(Source: Petty & Brooks-Heath, 2003)

WEP is applied to all data above the 802.11b WLAN layers (Physical and Data Link Layers, the first two layers of the OSI Reference Model[6]) to protect traffic such as Transmission Control Protocol/Internet Protocol (TCP/IP), Internet Packet Exchange (IPX) and Hyper Text Transfer Protocol (HTTP). It should be noted that only the frame body of data frames are encrypted and the entire frame of other frame types are transmitted in the clear, unencrypted (Karygiannis & Owens).

To add an additional integrity check, an Initialisation Vector (IV) is used in conjunction with the secret encryption key. The IV is used to avoid encrypting multiple consecutive ciphertexts with the same key, and is usually 24 bits long. The shared key and the IV are fed into the RC4 algorithm to produce the key stream. This is

---

[6] The OSI Reference Model is a 7-layer approach which separates the various functions of a network into specific parts; these are physical, data link, transmission, session, presentation and application.

XORed with the data to produce the ciphertext, the IV is then appended to the message. The IV of the incoming message is used to generate the key sequence necessary to decrypt the incoming message. The ciphertext, combined with the proper key sequence, yields the original plaintext and integrity check value (ICV) (Tyrrell, 2003). The decryption is verified by performing the integrity check algorithm on the recovered plaintext and comparing the output ICV to the ICV transmitted with the message. If it is in error, an indication is sent back to the sending station.

The IV increases the key size, for example, a 104 bit WEP key with a 24bit IV becomes a 128 bit RC4 key. In general, increasing the key size increases the security of a cryptographic technique. Research has shown that key sizes of greater than 80 bits make brute force[7] code breaking extremely difficult. For an 80 bit key, the number of possible keys - 10^{24} which puts computing power to the test; but this type of computing power is not beyond the reach of most hackers. The standard key in use today is 64-bit.

However, research has shown that the WEP approach to privacy is vulnerable to certain attacks regardless of key size. A report written by John Walker of Intel Corporation in 2000, called 'Unsafe at any key size; An analysis of the WEP encapsulation', proves this theory (Karygiannes & Owens). It would seem that WEP does not appear to have been subjected to a significant amount of peer review before it was released. Serious security flaws are present in the protocol. Although the application of WEP may stop casual 'sniffers', determine hackers can crack WEP keys in a busy network within a relatively short period of time.

---

[7] A method that relies on sheer computing power to try all possibilities until the solution to a problem is found, usually refers to cracking passwords by trying every possible combination of a particular key space.

3.3 WEP's Weaknesses

WEP's major weaknesses relate to three main issues. Firstly, the use of static keys, secondly, the length of the IV, and thirdly, the RC4 algorithm. Each will be examined in turn.

3.3.1 Static Keys

When WEP is enabled in accordance with the 802.11b standard, the network administrator must personally visit each wireless device in use and manually enter the appropriate WEP key. This may be acceptable at the installation stage of a WLAN or when a new client joins the network, but if the key becomes compromised and there is a loss of security, the key <u>must</u> be changed. This may not be a huge issue in a small organisation with only a few users, but it can be impractical in large corporations, who typically have hundreds of users (Dismukes, 2002). As a consequence, potentially hundreds of users and devices could be using the same, identical, key for long periods of time. All wireless network traffic from all users will be encrypted using the same key; this makes it a lot easier for someone listening to traffic to crack the key as there are so many packets being transmitted using the same key. Unfortunately, there were no key management provisions in the original WEP protocol.

3.3.2 IV Length

This is a 24 bit initialisation vector WEP appends to the shared key. WEP uses this combined key and IV to generate the RC4 key schedule; it selects a new IV for each packet, so each packet can have a different key. This forms a family of 2^{24} keys. As described, each packet transmission selects one of these 2^{24} keys and encrypts the data under that key. On the surface, this may appear to strengthen protection by lengthening the 40 bit WEP key, however this scheme suffers from a basic problem; if IVs are chosen randomly there is a 50% chance of reuse after less than 5,000 packets (Walker, 2000). The problem is a numerical restriction; because the IV is only 24 bits long, there are a finite number of variations of the IV for RC4 to pick from. Mathematically there are only 16,777,216 possible values for the IV. This may seem like a huge number, but given that it takes so many packets to transmit useful data, 16 million packets can easily go by in hours on a heavily used network. Eventually the RC4 algorithm starts using the same IVs over and over. Thus, someone passively 'listening' to encrypted traffic and picking out the repeating IVs can begin to deduce what the WEP key is. Made easier by the fact that there is a static variable, (the shared key), an attacker can eventually crack the WEP key. (iLabs, 2002)

For example, a busy AP, which constantly sends 1500 byte packets at 11Mbps, will exhaust the space of IVs after 1500 x 8/(11 x 10^6) x 2^24 = 18,000 seconds, or 5 hours. (The amount of time may actually be smaller since many packets are less than 1500 bytes). This allows an attacker to collect two ciphertexts that are encrypted with the same key stream. This reveals information about both messages. By XORing two ciphertexts that use the same key stream would cause the key stream to be cancelled out and the result would be the XOR of the two plaintexts (Vines, 2002). There is an additional problem that involves the use of IVs, more specifically, weak IVs. Some numbers in the range 0-16,777,215 don't work to well with the RC4 algorithm. When these weak IVs are used, the resulting packet can be run through a series of mathematical functions to decipher part of the WEP key. This weakness was famously highlighted by Flurer, Martin and Shamir in their paper, 'Weaknesses in the Key Scheduling Algorithm of RC4'. By capturing a large number of packets an attacker can pick out enough weak IVs to reveal the WEP key (PCQuest, 2003). Tools like Airsnort, which will be utilised in the primary research, specifically exploit this vulnerability to allow hackers to obtain the above information relatively easily. The crack process within Airsnort works by collecting packets thought to have been encrypted using a weak IV and then sorting them according to which key byte they help expose. A weak IV can assist in exposing only one key byte. The Flurer, et al, attack states that a weak IV has about a 5% chance of exposing the corresponding key byte. So, when a sufficient number of weak IVs have been collected for a particular key byte, statistical analysis will show a tendency towards a particular value for that key byte. The crack process makes a key guess based on the highest ranking values in the statistical analysis. Tests conducted by Stubblefield, et al, show that between 60 and 256 weak IVs were needed to recover a key (AirSnort FAQ).

In addition to the fundamental weaknesses in the WEP security protocol, (which is the primary security measure in WLANs), there are numerous other attacks that can be instigated against WLANs and their devices. Each of these will be discussed in turn in the next chapter; how they are carried out and what impact they could have. Some of these attacks will be carried out against the test WLAN as part of the primary research; this will assess the relative ease with which these attacks can be carried out and how effective they are.

3.4 War-Driving

A new 'sport' has emerged within the computer hacking world which takes advantage of some of the security weaknesses in WLANs. So called 'War-Driving' is a term used to describe a hacker, who, armed with a laptop, a wireless NIC, an antenna and sometimes a GPS device travels, usually by car, scanning or 'sniffing' for WLAN devices, or more specifically unprotected or 'open' and easily accessed networks . The name is thought to have come from another hacking technique called War-Dialling, where a hacker programs their system to call hundreds of phone numbers in search of a poorly protected computer dial-up (Poulsen, 2001). The concept is made possible by the way these devices interact and communicate with each other. All a hacker needs to do is move about from one place to another and let the devices do the rest. Over time, the hacker builds up a database of logged devices. Indeed there exists a web site where war-drivers can upload any information they obtain, the site is called Wigle and can be found at http://www.wigle.net (Vines, 2002).

Based on US anecdotal evidence just over a year ago, as many as 60-80 per cent of wireless LANs hadn't had the most basic steps taken to secure them, leaving them wide open to unauthorised third parties (Descoeudres, 2002). In November 2001, the BBC took to the streets of London to observe how lax wireless security was. In one short trip around London they found that two-thirds of the networks discovered were wide open (BBC News, 2001). It was noted some of the networks were using DHCP[8], making it even easier for an unauthorised individual to join the network, because they are automatically issued with a valid IP address and other network information. Due to the increased use of WLANs in recent years, it is quite possible that the number of unsecured devices has also risen in tandem, thus providing potential hackers with more choice. In July 2003, a reporter for PC Magazine took his tablet PC out to Madison Square Park

---

[8] Dynamic Host Control Protocol; governs the dynamic allocation of IP addresses to network devices/clients. (Easynet.com)

to see what he could pick up. Not surprisingly, he discovered a number of insecure networks he could hop on without any sort of ID, WEP encryption or even an SSID. After all that has been written about the insecurities of WLAN, some users/organisations still insist on implementing them with their default settings and no encryption (Ulanoff, 2003).

TOOL NAME	DESCRIPTION
Netstumbler http://www.netstumbler.com	Wireless AP identifier; listens for SSIDs and sends beacons as probes searching for APs.
Kismet http://kistmetwireless.net	Wireless sniffer and monitor; passively monitors wireless traffic and sorts data to identify SSIDs, MAC addresses, channels and connection speeds. Also identifies data with weak ICs that can be used by Airsnort to crack WEP.
Wellenreiter http://www.wellenreiter.net	LAN discovery tool; uses brute force to identify low traffic APs, hides real MAC address and integrates with GPS.
THC-RUT http://packetstormsecurity.nl/filedesc/thcrut-1.2.5.tar.html	WLAN discovery tool; uses brute force to identify low traffic APs.
Ethereal http://www.ethereal.com	Network analyser; interactively browses the captured data, viewing summary and detail information for all observed network traffic.
WEPCrack http://wepcrack.sourceforge.net	Encryption breaker; cracks 802.11 WEP encryption keys using the discovered weaknesses of the RC4 key scheduling.
AirSnort http://airsnort.shmoo.com	Encryption breaker; passively monitoring transmissions, computing the encryption key when enough packets have been gathered with weal IVs.
HostAP http://hostap.epitest.fi	Converts a WLAN station to function as an AP (available only for WLAN cards that are based on Intersil's Prism 2/2.5/3 chipset.

Table 1: Wireless Network Hacking Tools

(Source: SyDisTyKMoFo)

32

A Worldwide WarDrive, held in August to September 2002, discovered that 70% of APs were running without using any encryption, worse still 27% were doing so while using the default SSID that came with the hardware, leaving them wide open for use by anyone in range with a wireless NIC and a note of all vendor's default SSIDs.

These figures are rather disturbing figures; leaving an AP at its default settings is the this is the equivalent of putting an Ethernet socket on the outside of the building so anyone passing by can plug into the network (Griffith, October 2002). There are a range of hacking tools widely available to download from the Internet for any potential War-Driver to use. Table 1 contains some of the more popular tools and a brief description of their function.

There has been a lot of press and many articles written about wireless networks and their security vulnerabilities. Despite all this, some enterprises still make the mistake of believing that they don't have to worry about wireless security if they are running non-critical systems with non-sensitive information across their WLANs. All information is sensitive information, and what an enterprise may class as being non-sensitive to them may be very useful to a hacker. In addition, most WLANs will connect with the wired enterprise backbone at some point, thus providing hackers with a launch pad to the entire network. The havoc an unwelcome third party could cause from here would be unlimited and very difficult to trace. Aside from the various attacks they could instigate (DoS and viruses); the loss of confidentiality, privacy and integrity that would occur if someone where able to steal, alter or delete information on your customer database is damaging enough. Access to sensitive information would be made relatively easy, perhaps even customer's credit card details. This could have an un-quantifiable affect on business, perhaps resulting in the loss of customers/clients and future revenue (AirDefense, 2003).

4 Forms of Attack

This chapter deals with the various attacks that can be performed against WLANs (aside from the WEP crack), how they are carried out and what affect they have in relation to authentication, confidentiality and integrity, the three basic security requirements within networks. All of the attacks can be categorised into two general attack types; passive and active.

4.1 Passive Attacks

A passive attack is an attack on a system that does not result in a change to the system in any way; the attack is purely to monitor or record data. Passive attacks affect confidentiality, but not necessarily authentication or integrity. Eavesdropping and Traffic Analysis fall under this category. When an attacker eavesdrops, they simply monitor transmissions for message content. It usually takes the form of someone listening into the transmissions on a LAN between stations/devices (IT Glossary, 2003).

4.1.1 Eavesdropping

Eavesdropping is also known as 'sniffing' or wireless 'footprinting'. As mentioned in a previous chapter there are various tools available for download online which allow the monitoring of networks and their traffic; developed by hackers, for hackers. Netstumbler, Kismet, Airsnort, WEPCrack and Ethereal are all well known names in wireless hacking circles, and all are designed specifically for use on wireless networks, with the exception of Ethereal, which is a packet analyser and can also be used on a wired LAN. NetStumbler and Kismet can be used purely for passive eavesdropping; they have no additional active functions, except perhaps their ability to work in conjunction with Global Positioning Systems (GPSs) to map the exact locations of identified wireless

LANs. NetStumbler is a Windows-based sniffer, where Kismet is primarily a Linux-based tool.

NetStumbler uses an 802.11 Probe Request sent to the broadcast destination address, which causes all APs in the area to issue an 802.11 Probe Response containing network configuration information, such as their SSID, WEP status (not the WEP key!), the MAC address of the device, name (if applicable), the channel the device is transmitting on, the vendor and the type, either peer or AP, along with a few other pieces of information. Using the network information and GPS data collected, it is then possible to create maps with tools such as StumbVerter and MS Mappoint (McClure, et al, 2003). Kismet, although not as graphical or user friendly as NetStumbler, is similar to its Windows counterpart, but it provides superior functionality. While scanning for APs, packets can also be logged for later analysis. Logging features allow for captured packets to be stored in separate categories, depending upon the type of traffic captured. Kismet can even store encrypted packets that use weak keys separately to run them through a WEP key cracker after capture, such as Airsnort or WEPCrack (Sutton, 2002).

Wireless network GPS information can be uploaded to a site called Wigle (http://www.wigle.net). Therefore, if wigle data exists for a particular area, there is no need to drive around that area probing for wireless devices; this information can be obtained in advance from the Wigle web site. All that remains is to drive to a location where known networks exist to observe traffic. Wigle currently has a few hundred thousand networks on its database. See Appendix V for a sample of the kind of information available on the site.

4.1.2 Traffic Analysis

Traffic Analysis gains intelligence in a more subtle way by monitoring transmissions for patterns of communication. A considerable amount of information is contained in the flow of messages between communicating parties. Airopeek NX, a commercial 802.11 monitoring and analysis tool for Windows, analyses transmissions and provides a useful node view, which groups detected stations and devices by their MAC address and will also show IP addresses and protocols observed for each. The Peer Map view, within Airopeek NX, presents a matrix of all hosts discovered on the network by their connections to each other. This can make it very easy to visualise AP and client relationships, which could be useful to hackers in deciding where to try and gain access or target for an attack (McClure, et al, 2003).

Some attacks may begin as passive, but and then cross over to active as they progress. For example, tools such as Airsnort or WEPCrack may passively monitor transmissions, but their intent is to crack the WEP key used to encrypt data being transmitted. Ultimately the reasons for wanting to crack the key are so that an unauthorised individual can access a protected network and then launch an active attack of some form or another. These types of attack are classed as passive decryption attacks. Airsnort, mentioned previously, exploits the key weaknesses and uses this to crack WEP keys, as does WEPCrack. These are tools that put hackers on the first step towards an active attack. However, WEPCrack, unlike Airsnort, must be used in conjunction with a separate packet sniffer as it does not have the ability to capture network traffic.

These tools utilise what is known as a Brute Force technique to break codes. Brute Force is a method of breaking a cipher by trying every possible key until the correct key is found. The feasibility of this attack depends on the key length of the cipher, and/or the amount of computational power available to the attacker, and of course time. Another type of passive decryption attack is what is known as a Dictionary Attack, also a form of the brute force technique. A Dictionary Attack refers to breaking a cipher, or obtaining a password by running through a list of likely keys, or a list of words. The term Dictionary Attack initially referred to finding passwords in a specific list, such as an English dictionary. Today, a Brute Force approach can compute likely passwords, such as all five-letter combinations, 'on-the-fly' instead of using a pre-built list. The last Brute Force, passive decryption, attack is called a Table Attack and can be demonstrated with an example that makes reference to IVs. It is a method which involves using the relatively small number of IVs (24 bit) to build decryption tables. Once the contents of a single encrypted packet are known, the hacker can work backwards and build a table of all the keys possible with a particular IV (Franklin, 2001).

4.2 Active Attacks

An active attack, also referred to as a malicious attack, occurs when an unauthorised third party gains access to a network and proceeds to perform Denial of Service (DoS) attack, to disrupt the proper operation of a network, to intercept network traffic and either modify or delete it, or inject extra traffic onto the network. There are many active attacks that can be launched against wireless networks; the following few paragraphs outline almost all of these attacks, how they work and what affect they have (Karygiannis & Owens).

DoS attacks are easily the most prevalent type of attack against 802.11 networks, and can be waged against a single client or an entire WLAN. In this type of attack the hacker usually does not steal information, they simply prevent users from accessing network services, or cause services to be interrupted or delayed. Consequences can range from a measurable reduction in performance to the complete failure of the system. Some common DoS attacks are outlined below.

4.2.1   Man-in-the-Middle (MITM) Attack

This attack is carried out by inserting a malicious station between the victim station and the AP, thus the attacker becomes the 'man in the middle'; the station is tricked into believing that the attacker is the AP, and the AP into believing that the attacker is the legitimate station.

To being the attack the perpetrator passively monitors the frames sent back and forth between the station and the AP during the initial association process with an 802.11 analyser. As a result, information is obtained about both the station and the AP, such as the MAC and IP address of both devices, association ID for the station and SSID of the network. With this information a rogue station/AP can be set up between the two unsuspecting devices. Because the original 802.11 does not provide mutual authentication, a station will happily re-associate with the rogue AP. The rogue AP will then capture traffic from unsuspecting users, this of course can expose information such as user names and passwords.

After gleaning enough information about a particular WLAN, a hacker can then use a rogue station to mimic a valid one. This enables the hacker to deceive an AP by disassociating the valid station and reassociating again as a rogue station with the same parameters as the valid station. Two wireless cards are typically required for this type of attack (Wi-FiPlanet, Sept 2002). Once the attacker has successfully inserted themselves between the AP and client station, they are free to modify traffic, selectively forward or even delete it completely, while logging every packet that comes through it. In addition, the attacker is also free to explore and use other areas of the network as a legitimate user.

4.2.2   Session Hijacking

In this attack the intruder makes it appear to a legitimate user, who has just connected with the AP, that they've been disconnected. Much like the second half of the MITM attack, the intruder then connects with the still active WLAN connection, thereby hijacking the session.

The attacker must wait until the client has successfully authenticated to the network, then send a disassociate message to the client on the legitimate APs behalf, using the MAC address of the AP, then send frames to the valid AP, using the MAC address of the valid client.

However, this attack assumes that no encryption is present, otherwise the radio perpetrating the attack would not be able to gain access to the network after the hijack because the AP would reject all packets that do not match an encryption key corresponding to a known user, unless of course the attacker has taken the time beforehand to crack the key. When no encryption is present, this attack will easily succeed, allowing the attacker to use the session until the next reauthentication takes place. At the next reauthentication, the attacker would not be reauthenticated and effectively kicked-off, they would then have to hijack another valid session (Proxim, 2003).

4.2.3   MAC Spoofing – AKA Identity Theft

To carry off this attack the intruder impersonates a legitimate device on the network by stealing their credentials. To do this the attacker must change the manufacturer-assigned MAC identity of their NIC to the same value as a legitimate user on the network; they assume the identity of this user by spoofing their MAC address. By analysing traffic, a hacker can easily pick off MAC addresses of authorised users. The hacker then connects to the wireless LAN as an authorised user.

Somewhat similar in principal to the initial stage of the MITM attack, where a device impersonates or masquerades as someone they are not. This attack enables the hacker to transmit and receive data within the network as an authorised member; because they are using the identity of an authorised user it will hide their presence on the network and bypass any MAC address-based ACLs (Wright, 2003).

See Appendix VI for details on how to change the MAC address manually on a Windows XP-based PC, and details on where to download a copy of SMAC, a MAC modifying utility.

4.2.4   Other MAC Vulnerabilities

A utility known as Interframe spacing can also be utilised to launch malicious attacks, see Appendix VII for a definition and details on Interframe spacing. Since every transmitting node must wait at least the Shortest Interframe Space (SIFS) interval before transmitting, if not longer, an attacker could completely monopolise the channel by sending a short signal just before the end of every SIFS period. While this attack could be highly effective, it also requires the attacker to expel considerable energy; an SIFS period is only 20 microseconds on 802.11b networks, leading to a cycle of 50,000 packets per second in order to disable all access to a network (Bellardo and Savage, 2003).

However, a more serious vulnerability arises from the virtual carrier-sense mechanism used to mitigate collisions from hidden terminals[9]. For a definition of the hidden terminal problem. Each 802.11 frame carries a Duration Field that indicates the number of microseconds that the channel is reserved. This value, in turn, is used to program the Network Allocation Vector (NAV) on each node. The NAV keeps stations quiet until the first acknowledgement of a transmission is received. Only when a node's NAV reaches zero is it allowed to transmit. This feature is principally used in the Ready-to-Send/Clear-to-Send (RTS/CTS) handshake that can be used to synchronise access to the channel when a hidden terminal may be interfering with transmissions.

During this handshake the sending node first sends a small RTS frame that includes a duration large enough to complete the RTS/CTS sequence, including the CTS frame, the data frame, and the subsequent ACK frame. The destination node replies to the RTS with a CTS, containing a new NAV value, updated to account for the time already elapsed in the sequence.

After the CTS is sent every station in radio range of either the sending or receiving station will have updated their NAV and will hold all transmissions for the defined duration. While the RTS/CTS feature is rarely used in practice, respecting the virtual carrier sense function indicated by the NAV field is mandatory in all 802.11 implementations.

An attacker may exploit this feature by stating a large duration field, thereby preventing stations from gaining

---

[9] A problem that occurs when one, or more, stations cannot 'hear' all other stations. These stations cause collisions by transmitting at the same time as another station.

access to the channel. While it is possible to use almost any frame type to control the NAV, using the RTS with CTS, legitimate stations will propagate the attack further than it could on its own by passing the large NAV value to all stations within range. To cause a noticeable degradation in network performance, this attack can be carried out again and again, to disrupt network functioning, resulting in a DoS (Bellardo and Savage).

4.2.5   Malicious Association

Using a freeware tool called HostAP to create what is known as a 'Soft AP', hackers can force unsuspecting stations to connect to an undesired 802.11 network or alter the configuration of the station to operate in ad-hoc mode. The HostAP software enables a station to operate as a functioning AP. As the victim station broadcasts a probe to associate with an AP, the attacker's malicious AP responds and starts a connection between the two.

At this time, the attacker can exploit the vulnerable victim station. It could be used as a launch pad to the rest of the network, viruses could be unleashed and a so called backdoor could be left for later use. This attack is highlights how vulnerable client stations are; they are not always aware that the AP they connect to is legitimate, this can be attributed to the lack of mutual authentication (SyDisTyKMoFo).

4.2.6   De-authentication

Part of the communications framework between an 802.11 AP and client is a message which allows them to explicitly issue a request for de-authentication from one another at any stage. Even if some form of key authentication does exist, this message is not authenticated, which makes it relatively simple for a third party to spoof this message on behalf of either device and direct it to the other party. In response, the AP or client will exit the authenticated state and will refuse all further packets until authentication is re-established. By repeating the attack persistently a client may be kept from transmitting or receiving data indefinitely (Bellardo & Savange).

4.2.7   Association Flood

This is a resource starvation attack. When a station associates with an AP, the AP issues an Associate Identification number (AID) to the station in the range of 1-2007. This value is used for communicating power management information to a station that has been in a power-save state. This attack works by sending multiple authentication and association requests to the AP, each with a unique source MAC address. The AP is unable to differentiate the authentication requests generated by an attacker and those created by legitimate clients, so it is forced to process each request.

Eventually, the AP will run out of AIDs to allocate and will be forced to de-associate stations to reuse previously allocated AIDs. In practice, many APs will restart after a few minutes of authentication flooding, however this attack is effective in bringing down entire networks or network segments; if repeatedly carried out, can cause a noticeable decrease in network up time (Wright, May 2003).

4.2.8   Power Save Vulnerability

Much like a PC or laptop enters stand-by mode after a period of inactivity, a client station within a WLAN is also permitted to enter a stand-by state, known as power save mode. In this state clients are unable to transmit or receive. Before entering power save mode the client is required to announce its intention so that the AP can start buffering any inbound traffic for the node. Occasionally, the client will awaken to poll the AP for any traffic destined for it. If there is any buffered data, the AP delivers it and subsequently discards the contents of its buffer. By spoofing the polling message on behalf of the client, an attacker can cause the AP to discard the client's packets while it is in power save mode. Along the same lines, it is potentially possible to trick the client station into thinking there are no buffered packets at the AP when in fact there are. The presence of buffered packets is indicated in a periodically broadcast packet called the Traffic Indication Map, or TIM. If the TIM message itself is spoofed, an attacker may convince a client that there is no buffered data for it and the client will immediately revert back to stand-by state (Bellardo & Savage).

4.2.9   Jamming

Jamming is a ridiculously simple, yet highly effective method of causing a DoS on a wireless LAN. Jamming, as the name suggests, involves the use of a device to intentionally create interfering radio signals to effectively 'jam' the airwaves, resulting in the AP and any client devices being unable to transmit. Unfortunately 802.11b WLANs are easily jammed – intentionally or otherwise – due to the crowded frequency band that they operate in. This provides a would-be attacker with plenty of opportunity, and tools, to jam wireless network signals (Computer Associates, 2003).

4.2.10   The Michael Vulnerability

This attack exploits a weakness in the Wi-Fi Alliance's Protected Access Protocol (WPA). Michael is the codename for a security function within the TKIP encryption system used by WPA; this security function triggers the AP to shutdown if more than two packets of unauthorised data are received during a one-second period. The rationale behind the shutdown is to protect the network from attack; the AP assumes it is under attack and takes the proactive measure of shutting down to prevent any potential attacker from entering the network (Stone, 2002). This shut-down is supposed to thwart attack, but in itself it is a means of attack. A attacker could send vast quantities of unauthorised data, thus triggering an ongoing series of shut-downs. This type of attack is unique to WPA, is easy to mount, and is very stealthy in that only two packets need to be sent every second. Even with sophisticated direction finding equipment it would be difficult to track down the perpetrator.

4.3 Attacks that Alter Transmissions

The following attacks describe how it is possible for an attacker to modify messages in transit, without detection. Message modification attacks are made relatively trivial if no message encryption exists, however, even if it does, the hacker can still get around it by first cracking the encryption and then carrying out the attack.

4.3.1 Injecting Traffic

If an attacker knows the exact plaintext for one encrypted message, they can then use this knowledge to construct more correctly encrypted packets. This procedure involves constructing a new message, calculating the CRC-32 checksum, and performing bit-flips[10] on the original encrypted message to change the plaintext to the new message. This packet can now be sent to the AP, and it will be accepted as a valid packet. Because RC4 encrypts data a byte at a time, an attacker can modify one byte of ciphertext and the recipient would not know the data has been changed. RC4 does not detect errors (Borisov, et al).

4.3.2 IP Redirection

By intercepting and modifying the IP address of the destination in a packet, an attacker can effectively re-route messages. This attack can be used where an AP acts as an IP router with Internet connectivity, which is fairly common. The idea is to take an encrypted packet that has been transmitted, modify it so it has a new destination address, one the attacker controls. The AP will then decrypt the packet and send it off to its new destination, where the attacker can read the packet, now in the clear (Borisov, et al).

---

[10] Bit-flipping – changing one or more bits within a message. For example, change a 0 to a 1, or vice versa. (Techweb.com)

4.3.3 SNMP Attack

The final issue is a threat posed by the Simple Network Management Protocol (SNMP). Some APs can be managed via wireless link, usually with a proprietary application, replying on SNMP. Executing these operations can represent a frightening vulnerability for the whole LAN; because eavesdroppers can decipher the password to access read/write mode on the AP using a packet analyser, this means that they share the same administration privileges with the WLAN administrator and can manage the WLAN in a malicious manner (Me, 2003).

The sheer number of attacks, and their affects, would seem to put WLANs at a severe disadvantage over their wired counterparts. However, there are just as many, if not more, security measures that users can utilise to counteract most of the above attacks. Layering one security measure on top of another, to strengthening the overall system to deter any potential attackers, or make their task more difficult, if not impossible.

However, as noted in a previous chapter, not all organisations, or indeed individuals, take the time to implement any form of security, or they implement it weakly.

5   War Driving & WiFi Hacking

The purpose of this chapter is to demonstrate how easy it will be for rogue persons to infiltrate those networks that we are charged with protecting. We outline the results of our war driving in the city of Londonderry, Northern Ireland during 2003. We present the results of how many of the WLANs were protected and how many were open as a percentage of the devices discovered. The investigation was carried out by driving around the target area, equipped with a Laptop, wireless NIC, an external antenna, and NetStumbler for Windows. This probed for any wireless devices in use within range and reported various details about the devices discovered. Association with open AP's was attempted as was obtaining an Internet connection by proxy. The information collected was used to produce the findings later in this chapter.

It must be stressed that the war driving was purely white-hat[11], no malicious attempts were made against any networks or devices discovered to be lacking in security, no further network penetration attempted either. This would have been unethical and defy the efforts of this book to identify weaknesses and present recommendations to help users.

With the equipment discussed in chapter one, (laptop, wireless NIC and GPS device), and the necessary software, (NetStumbler and Ethereal), a white-hat war-drive was undertaken. The rationale behind this research was to, firstly, discover how many wireless networks/devices were in use in this area, and secondly, observe if they had any security measures in place, namely WEP, or if they were open to attack.

Without further network probing it is unclear what other security measures users had in place other than or in addition to WEP. This information was not immediately

---

[11] A white hat describes a hacker who identifies a security weakness in a computer system but, instead of taking malicious advantage of it, exposes the weakness in a way that will allow the system's owners to fix the breach before it can be taken advantage of by others. (SearchSecurity.com Definitions)

available. For the purposes of this book it was assumed that when a device was displayed as being open on NetStumbler, it was deemed as having no security measures in place. When a device was displayed in NetStumbler as being protected by WEP, it was assumed that this was the only security measure they were utilising.

We also created our own WLAN lab environment using an AP and two PC's acting as a network with a third PC acting as an attacker. This is used to demonstrate how easy it is be for a potential attacker to gain access and cause damage. A selection of the attacks mentioned in previous chapters were attempted against the test network; the exact selection will be identified later in this chapter. This serves to illustrate the very real affects of various attacks and their consequences. The outcome of this research is applicable to the networks discovered in the first layer of research.

Over the period of three months, from August to October 2003, initial scans were carried out in the area. The first few scans were used to test the software and equipment to ensure they were operating correctly, verified by the same information being picked up in the second test as in this first, proving the consistency of the information collected. Table 2 displays the devices discovered over this period. It is worth noting at this stage that 30 devices were detected, out of which only a mere five were protected with WEP; however two of these were BTOpenZone Hotspots. A staggering 83% of the devices detected were open and vulnerable to attack. Even if security measures are implemented further into the network, the fact that the gateway is wide open enabling a connection to be made, provides the first step towards launching an attack.

#	MAC	SSID	DEFAULT	ENCRYPTION	CHANNEL	TYPE
1	0030AB099F8D	Wireless	YES	NO	6	AP
2	02D0D86402D0	Brieco Wireless Network	NO	YES-WEP	9	PEER
3	00022D20CBBD	WaveLAN Network	YES	NO	10	AP
4	0009B43173C	NETGEAR	NO	YES-WEP	11	AP
5	0002B3B140C8	101	NO	NO	11	AP
6	0007408BAB18	0007408B8CF8	NO	NO	11	AP
7	0209D16EF444	KYOCERA	NO	NO	3	PEER
8	00047562B639	3Com	NO	NO	1	AP
9	00ED18B29361	default	NO	NO	1	AP
10	000476A7A325	3Com	NO	NO	6	AP
11	4096366501	testlab	NO	NO	7	AP
12	0030AB0B711E	exuswlan27templemore	NO	YES-WEP	11	AP
13	00022D2DEB1C	WaveLAN Network	YES	NO	10,1,2,3,4,5,6,7	AP
14	0030650C7E30	MSHOME	NO	NO	11	UNKNOWN
15	022384D093A8	MSHOME	NO	NO	11	PEER
16	00601D23368C	ANY	NO	NO	6	AP
17	0030AB1E5CAB	Wireless	YES	NO	1	AP
18	000A417D4128	BTOpenzone	NO	NO	7	AP
19	022365DC93A8	MSHOME	NO	NO	11	PEER
20	0223EDD093A8	MSHOME	NO	NO	11	PEER
21	00022D2DDBF8	WaveLAN Network	YES	NO	10	AP
22	00022D1CF3A2	WaveLAN Network	YES	NO	10	AP
23	00022D285F63	WaveLAN Network	YES	NO	10	AP
24	00022D28616B	WaveLAN Network	YES	NO	10	AP
25	0009B4C1E46	Wireless	NO	NO	6	AP
26	000D549B774F	Singularity	NO	YES-WEP	10	AP
27	000D549B7FB4	Singularity	NO	YES-WEP	11	AP
28	0209563 9F444	KYOCERA	NO	NO	11,5	PEER
29	020939F7F444	KYOCERA	NO	NO	11	PEER
30	000A417D4128	BTOpenzone	NO	NO	7,1,10,4,3,11	AP

Table 2: Wireless Devices Discovered

With the exception of the BT Hotspots, internet access was gained through all open devices apart from the six devices with the WaveLAN Network SSID; obviously http traffic is disallowed on this network. These devices are deemed to be part of one overall network due to the similarity in SSID and GPS coordinates; all devices were sensed within a close geographical area within the grounds of one particular set of buildings.

The implications of an unknown third party having access to an Internet connection are huge. Because their presence online is disguised by the IP address of the connection they are using they can do whatever they want virtually undetected. This may appear harmless on the surface, but if this person were to use the connection to launch a series of Internet-based DoS attacks or a huge spam-mail campaign, or to use the connection to hack into another network, or worse still, to download and distribute explicit and/or illegal material, the implications could be far reaching. It may be difficult for the owner of the connection to disprove any allegations raised and the consequences could be disastrous. In addition to this, network performance could be affected. Users may notice a real degradation in network bandwidth if third parties are using the connection continuously for downloads. Users with internet-based applications may experience a noticeable reduction in performance, thereby affecting their ability to carry out their job. Even more disturbing, a total of eight out of the thirty devices discovered were operating under their default settings. This means that the devices were literally taken out of their boxes and plugged in, no further configuration was attempted. As mentioned, this is the equivalent of putting an Ethernet connection on the outside of the building, enabling anyone passing by to join the network.

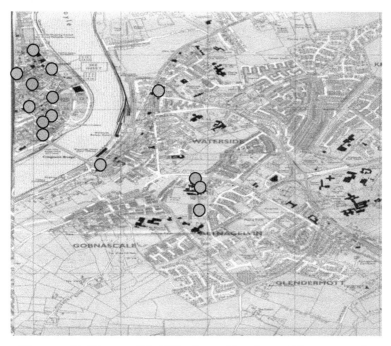

Figure 5: Map with Wireless Devices Discovered

The five remaining devices were locked using WEP encryption. The weaknesses of WEP were discussed in chapter two, however, regardless of how weak WEP is, this encryption is a deterrent. Any potential hacker will have to spend time (depending on network traffic loads) outside a building collecting packets and running the risk of being caught. If these networks have relatively low traffic, WEP may be sufficient to protect them. It would take a potential hacker an unjustified length of time before enough packets could be collected to effectively crack the key.

Figure 5 depict a maps of the areas where devices where discovered in the war-drive. The devices have been plotted on the map as a series of coloured dots. A red dot represents a locked device and a green dot represents an unprotected device. The overwhelming number of greens dots is apparent when plotted in this manner. However, if the network has a heavy traffic load, WEP may not be effective; also mentioned in chapter two, five hours may be all it would take to collect enough packets, less if packets are small and there is considerable traffic.

5.1 Security Testing in Lab

To further test WiFi security weaknesses, we also set up a test bed WiFi network. The test bed network consisted of one AP, two workstations with a wireless NICs, and one third-party workstation acting as attacker. The purpose is to demonstrate how easy it would be for an attacker to gain access to a wireless network and the damage they could cause. This will apply to all the devices discovered in the previous section.

During this testing a selection of attacks were conducted to assess their simplicity and effectiveness. Full network penetration was attempted and a detailed explanation is provided for each attempt. For security purposes, the test network was at no time connected to a wired backbone as this would represent a major security issue for the network concerned. It must be noted that the tests performed were be restricted by the functionality of the test hardware. This, in turn, directly impacted upon the selection of attacks that could be attempted. Please refer to Appendix VIII for a detailed list of equipment used. The AP used offers a few security options; these are WEP at varying key lengths, MAC-address-based filtering and SSID hiding.

Experiments were run to test the effectiveness of the WEP security protocol as this is what the devices identified in the area are using as protection, along with a few other basic security measures. Airsnort will be used to test WEP, and Ethereal and SMAC will be used to penetrate the MAC filtering and SSID hiding. The relative success or otherwise of these techniques will be discussed along with details of the relative ease with which they were executed. In addition to this, the SNMP attack was also attempted to demonstrate how easy it would be for an attacker to gain access and reconfigure the APs identified in the live networks earlier; made even easier by the lack of security.

It is assumed that some level of file and service sharing is set up between clients in the live networks as this is the prime rationale for networking, to share resources. Therefore, within the test network a few of the folders on the drive of each PC have been shared for access by other members of the network, as has the printer service. The nature of files and folders that are typically shared within a network are files that everyone requires access to either for leisure or for business. This could be films or photographs in the home environment or business related documents and records, for example, accounting and customer information, within the office environment.

Occasionally whole hard drives are carelessly shared instead of selective folders or files, which is much more than is required. This provides access to everything on the shared PC, including sensitive Operating System files the PC needs in order to function; Windows, for example.

For home users, the nature of shared files may not carry the same level of sensitivity, but the dangers are much the same. If the entire hard drive is shared, this leaves the PC vulnerable to changes and the Operating System files are exposed to deletion or alteration. To imitate the real networks discovered in our war driving, the first level of security was no security. No attacks are required to gain access to an open network. Information obtained from NetStumbler is enough for this. Just a few configuration changes on the PC will allow association with the AP and thus participation in the network.

Subsequent to this, a demonstration and description of the damage that could be caused to a network with this type of easy access will be detailed. This will be applicable to those apparently open networks discovered in the Londonderry area. Further attacks are made trivial in environments like this as there is no need to break through any security in order to execute them. These attacks are also possible after the WEP key has been compromised. For each of these attacks carried out a brief description is provided detailing whether or not the attack was successful and how successful it is deemed with respect to the time it took to perform and the relative ease with which is was executed.

5.2 Levels of Security Categorisation

Each of the security options mentioned here will be touched upon in more detail in the recommendations section later. Definition of levels are as follows:

Light

Easily broken or bypassed

- Changing SSID
- Disabling SSID broadcasts
- Changing default settings on AP
- Enabling MAC filtering
- Enabling WEP

Medium

Tougher than light, but not impossible to break

- WPAv1

Heavy

Strong security, hard if not impossible to break

- WPAv2
- VPNs
- IDSes

The tools that will be utilised within the lab-style research are NetStumbler, Ethereal, AirSnort and SMAC. The hardware includes three laptop PC's; one Windows/Linux-based, two Windows-based, three wireless NIC's; one with Prism II chipset and one Buffalo Access Point (AP).

5.3 Attack 1 – Joining an Unsecured Network

The screen shot in Figure 6 'WIRELESSOFFICE', detected by NetStumbler contained enough information to enable a PC to be configured to use the WIRELESSOFFICE connection and then join the WIRELESSOFFICE network. Once an intruder has access they will have the same privileges as legitimate users on the network if no security is in place. If any files/folders are shared on any connected PC's the intruder will have access to these also. They will be able to copy, delete or move these files/folders, with devastating consequences. They are also free to implement any of the attacks mentioned in chapter three.

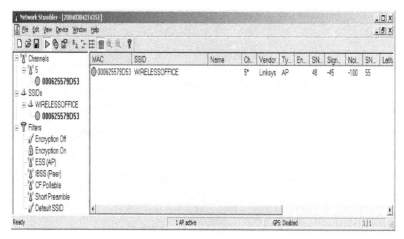

Figure 6: NetStumbler Showing Test Network

The hard drive of the PC's in the test network were shared in full. This meant that both PC's were able to browse, copy, change or delete files on the other. This also meant that the third PC, acting as intruder, was also able to browse, copy, change or delete the files and folders on the two PC's. If an internet connection had been available through the AP, the third PC would also have been able to use this.

56

5.4 Attack 2 – Joining a Network with MAC-Filtering

Next, MAC address-based filtering was enabled on the AP allowing access to only one of the PC's using the hardware MAC address on the wireless NIC. This was verified by the connection on the disallowed PC going down and the connection on the authorised PC coming back up again. The MAC address information was easily obtained using Ethereal packet analyser.

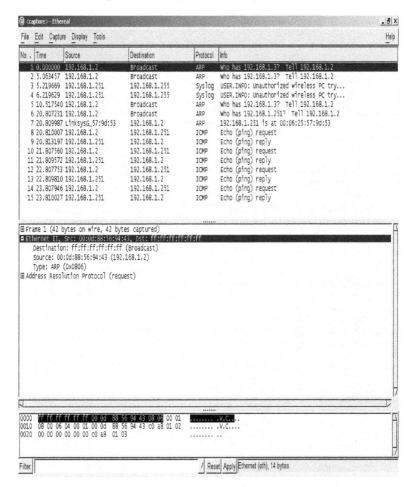

Figure 7: Screen Shot from Ethereal

The screen shot in Figure 7 shows the MAC address of the authorised card highlighted in blue. This information was then used to change the MAC address on the other PC to match that of an authorised user. This was done using SMAC, a MAC address changing utility provided by KLC Consulting.

Figure 8 provides a sample screen from SMAC showing the original MAC address and the spoofed MAC address.

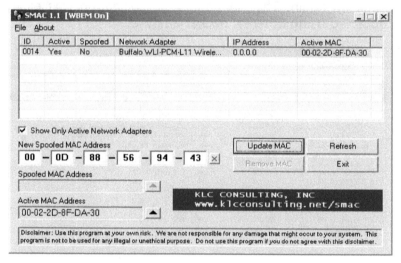

Figure 8: Screen Shot from SMAC

After the PC was restarted it assumed the MAC address of the authorised PC and was permitted to join the network by the AP. The two screen shots in Figure 9 show the configuration of the PC before the MAC address change and afterwards.

Before:

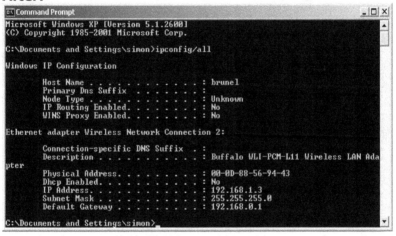

After:

Figure 9: Screen Shots of Card Identity

Note the Physical Address has changed on the Buffalo card and that it has been allowed to connect to the network by the AP. This proves just how weak this security method is. MAC address-based access lists are easy to penetrate. This whole exercise took under 10 minutes to implement, providing quick access to the target network using the minimum of tools and expertise.

5.5 Attack 3 - Joining a Network with SSID Hiding

Normally the SSID is broadcast by AP's so that cards within range can receive the necessary information to enable them to join the network. On some AP's this function can be disabled meaning that cards wanting to join the network must be configured beforehand with the SSID before they can join the network. With the right equipment and tools the SSID information is easily obtained in other messages that pass between the AP and its clients. NetStumbler will still report the network SSID and Ethereal also provided the network name within the first few packets (see Figure 10).

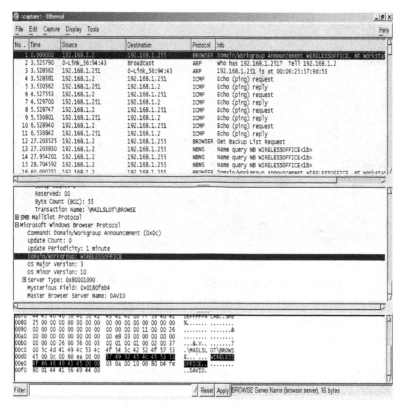

Figure 10: Ethereal Showing SSID

This is easily identifiable, even by the most inexperienced of users, as the first packet is a domain/workgroup announcement showing the SSID clearly. Needless to say that a connection can be made possible after this information has been gleaned. SSID hiding is not a strong method of denying access. It is also purported to affect network throughput (Moskowitz, 2003); however, establishing this proved difficult as two of the test network cards could not detect the AP after the SSID was hidden, therefore it could be said that SSID hiding affects network performance by causing connectivity issues but only on certain NICs.

This proved to be the weakest of the basic security options available to users, with network access being gained in a matter of minutes. However, without the use of NetStumbler and Ethereal there is no way of knowing what the SSID is unless one is a legitimate user of the network.

5.6 Attack 4 – Joining a Network with WEP Enabled

This is probably the strongest basic security measure available. WEP was enabled on the AP at 64-bits as this was the lowest key size allowed, 40 was not an option. The cards on the two test network PC's were also configured to use 64-bit WEP encryption. The key was based on a series of numbers, 3145324641, which produced a key of 17BE311175 – generated by the AP. This key was then used to configure the PC's. The third PC, acting as attacker, was not configured with the WEP key nor network information and was hence not part of the legitimate network. Instead it was left to run Airsnort on Linux Mandrake 9.1 and monitor all traffic passing over the WIRELESSOFFICE network. NetStumbler was used first to identify which channel the AP and clients were operating on; channel 5. Airsnort was then set to capture packets from this channel. This was a necessity as when Airsnort was set to scan and capture on all channels the system simply froze up and refused to operate.

The WIRELESSOFFICE network was detected as soon as the Airsnort capture began, it was also identified that WEP was in use. To speed the crack process up, files were copied between the two PC's in the network. This created network traffic for Airsnort to analyse.

After only two hours of traffic and around 4.9 million packets, Airsnort was able to crack the 64-bit key based on the information it had gathered. Figure 11 shows a screen shot of Airsnort showing the number of packets gathered and the WEP key, exactly as detailed above; 17BE311175.

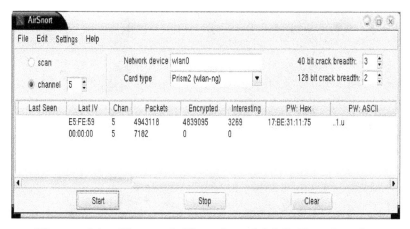

Figure 11: Airsnort Showing 64-bit Key Crack

Following this a 128-bit WEP was implemented to test the relative strength of using a longer key. This time the key was based on 314532464156, two digits more than previously, and produced the 26 long character sequence 053DB0F983E36FBF0B308627A2, just over two and a half times longer than the sequence produced by the 64-bit number series.

After approximately 6.2 million packets had passed over the network, Airsnort was able to provide the crack for the 128-bit key. Surprisingly fewer packets than anticipated. Figure 12 provides depicts the screen shot from this crack clearly showing the number of packets and the exact key.

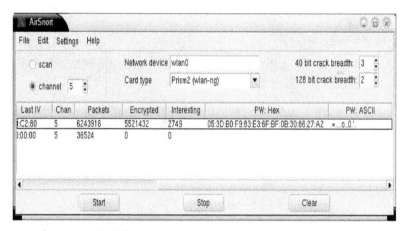

Figure 12: Airsnort Showing 128-bit Key Crack

Airsnort is highly effective in breaking WEP. Testing on a 256-bit key could not be carried out due to hardware limitations. However, on comparison of the number of packets taken to break the 64 and 128-bit keys, it is estimated that the 256-bit key would not take a huge number of packets before its key is also exposed. When WEP is broken an attacker is free to join a network protected in this manner. They can then carry out further attacks using the HostAP driver, like malicious association and de-association. Or worse still they can browse and copy networked files and folders. For the networks that are protected by WEP in the Londonderry area this is a very real threat. This all proves just how weak WEP is and the field research shows that of the networks that were protected in the region, all were using WEP.

Because Airsnort runs on a Linux-based PC it makes it one of the more tricky hacks to run, especially if coming from a Windows-based background. Airsnort is not easy to implement unless you know what you are doing. It is not easy to implement or to get running without some form of Linux knowledge. The wireless NIC requires special drivers to enable it to function under Linux, the wireless card must also have a certain chipset in order for it to be able to be instructed by the special drivers. This chipset is what is known as Prism II and not all cards use this chipset. Indeed it is quite difficult to find out information about a wireless card's chipset as this information does not appear on the manufacturer's packaging or documentation. The only way to determine a card's chipset is to perform searches online in Linux mail archives and related web sites. If the card is new it makes it even more problematic as information online usually relates to older cards that have been tried and tested.

Information on how to download, install and run Airsnort is included in Appendix IX, including the prism II drivers. Once Airsnort has been installed and is running it is relatively simple to use and quick to execute, it can be left to run with little effort required from the hacker. Because it is passive in nature, Airsnort can be run without fear of being detected, unless a network administrator is extremely observant.

5.7 Attack 5 – Network Admin Password

It is also possible to obtain the information required to gain access to the administrator privileges on the AP and thus make configuration changes which will affect network connectivity for the attached PC's. Using Ethereal packets were gathered as one of the client PC's logged onto the AP to make configuration changes. After examining Ethereal's output the required information was located within a short period of time in packet number 120.

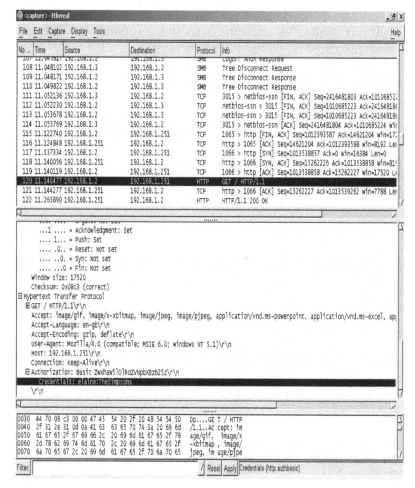

Figure 13: Ethereal Showing username & password

See the screens shot in Figure 13 and Figure 14 plainly show the administrator username and password; elaine and TheSimpsons. This information allows access to the configuration of the AP with network administrator's privileges. The IP address of the AP is also easily obtained from Ethereal, this is also required in order to connect to the AP using Internet Explorer.

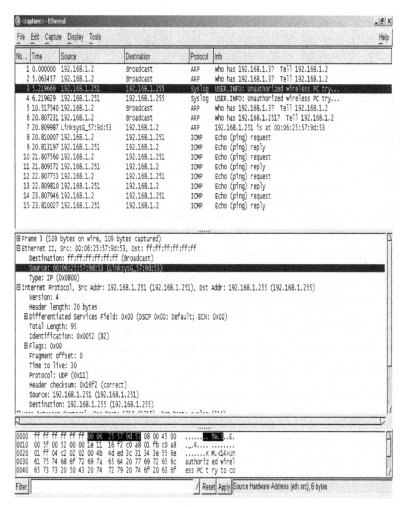

Figure 14: Ethereal Showing Username & Password

For the purposes of comparison and to aid the recommendations, a final test on network traffic was undertaken. This was to assess normal traffic levels and ascertain who long it may be before a certain number of packets was achieved on a network during normal use. Ethereal packet counts were used to gauge traffic loads in various situations within a ten minute period.

The varying situations were continuous traffic achieved by copying a file; intermittent traffic achieved by accessing, browsing, amending and saving files on one PC from the other; and, low traffic achieved by simply having a ten minute period of inactivity. This is to reflect and in some way simulate the traffic patterns of the three groups identified.

The home user would have large periods of inactivity and traffic loads in bursts usually in the early evening and more frequent at the weekends. This can be reflected by mixing part intermittent traffic and inactivity in the ratio of 20/80 based on a twelve hour day. For the small office traffic will be the same as continuous intermittent use throughout normal office hours and then have a large period of inactivity out of office hours. The ratio here would be 60/40 based on a twelve hour day, with 40 representing the period of inactivity.

Due to the sheer size of a medium to large organisation and the number of devices on the network, their traffic load can be best reflected by the continuous traffic load detailed above. Their usage will also be usually 60/40 in a twelve hour day, but can also extend towards a full twelve hour day of usage depending on the organisation.

Chapter 6 provides recommendations based on these findings.

5.8 Conclusion

As per the packet capture count on Airsnort approximately 31,471 packets past in a ten minute period when there was continuous traffic on the network. This is equal to 188,826 packets per hour. Using this as a benchmark the following estimations can be made:

To generate the 4,900,000 packets needed to crack the 64-bit key, around 26 hours of continuous traffic is required (4,900,000/(31,471*6)=25.9 hours). And to generate the 6,200,000 packets needed to crack the 128-bit key, around 33 hours of continuous traffic is required (6,200,000/(31,471*6)=32.8 hours).

The number of packets created by accessing a small word document on another PC created around 13,000 packets. If you multiply this by say 5 devices you get 65,000 packets produced on the network right away, simply by accessing a document on another computer in the network. 5 devices would be typical of the home office user group defined in the next chapter. The home user is deemed to have network traffic for a few hours at a time in the evening or during the day at the weekend. The amount of time that it would take to generate the 4.9 million packets for a 64-bit key crack and the 6.2 million packets for a 128-bit key crack could be calculated as follows:

If sharing files with another computer in the home, the number of packets generated by accessing a file, making a change and saving this change on the other computer created 6,600 packets. If this type of access is carried out approximately twice every ten minutes this would create 13,200 packets, totalling 79,200 packets per hour. Meaning that it would take around 62 hours to generate enough packets on the home network to enable a 64-bit key to be broken.

However, if the connection is being used to download films or music files over the internet continuously for hours this calculation will be different as the traffic will be more sustained and packet rich. Based on file sharing, a network with 20 end user devices all accessing files in a similar manner on a server in the network could create 1,584,000 packets per hour, meaning that a 64-bit key could be broken in around 3 hours. If accessing files more often than this or if there are more end users, the time taken to generate enough packets will decrease.

It must be noted that these are theoretical figures and that Airsnort has no set packet count for cracking various keys. In its documentation, the crack can occur quickly or it could take a long period of time. There is no definitive time period.

6 Securing a Wireless Network

There exists at present a serious lack of security on WiFi networks. Even those users that have implemented WEP may not realise just how weak this protocol can be. The following recommendations are aimed at each specific group of user; beginning with the home user, progressing to the SOHO group and medium to large organisations. The levels of security recommended will also progress due to the increasing security rating of each group.

6.1 Definitions and Assumptions

This section provides definitions for these groups and any associated assumptions. It must be noted that the classifications provided do not relate to turnover or any other business related metric, but simply based on common attributes like the number of devices employed and network traffic loads.

6.1.1 Home User

A user who typically uses one AP in their home in conjunction with one or more PCs (not more than three) to access the internet and provide coverage for their devices within their household. Network usage is solely for the purposes of leisure and does not relate to any form of business activity.

Home User Summary

Network usage: 100% leisure
Number of end-user devices: 1-2 (not more than 3)
Security Rating: low

6.1.2 SOHO User

A recognised market segment with many products and solutions specifically developed for them. This definition will probably differ from the market definition for this group. For the purposes of this book, this type of user is two-fold. The home office is located within the home premises, usually a room in the house or a building in the grounds. The small office is located away from the home premises and is either leased or owned and used solely for the purposes of business.

The home office user is deemed to have only one AP, depending on the size of the home, with three or more PCs (not more than five). For this group, network usage is part business, part leisure, with a ratio of typically 80/20% of time spent on each. The equipment is used mainly for the purposes of conducting business, but also as a home user for leisure. The small office segment of this group is defined as a leased/owned commercial office environment where four or more (not more than twenty) wireless devices are in use, not including APs. The number of APs in use can vary between one and three, depending on the area to be covered and the segregation required. Network usage is solely for the purposes of conducting business.

SOHO Summary

Network Usage: Home office, 80% business, 20% leisure
                     Small office, 100% business
End-User Devices: 4 or more (not more than 20)
Security Rating: Medium

6.1.3 Medium to Large Organisational User

Medium to large organisations are defined as operating more than twenty end-user devices. No upper limit on the number of devices has been defined; this will encompass all organisations larger than the small office. The rationale is that organisations with more than twenty end-user devices will have similar operational and security issues; therefore recommendations can be aimed at the group as a whole, rather than further dissection. Below is a summary of the user groups defined above. The security rating is an assumption that relates to the perceived attractiveness to attackers of each group's network; the home user being the least attractive and the medium to large organisation being the most attractive.

Medium to Large Organisations Summary

Network Usage: 100% business
Number of End User Devices: 20 or more, no upper limit
Security Rating: High

6.1.4 Summary of User Groups

The following recommendations are based on the findings presented in chapter four and upon which option is viewed to be most appropriate for each group of user. This is somewhat subjective and does not consider what type of applications each group of user will be using their WLAN for.; that is, type of application and consequent traffic load. It simply assumes that the home user will have relatively low traffic; the SOHO user will have moderate traffic levels, whereas the medium to large organisations will have considerable/heavy traffic loads, mainly due to the sheer number of devices in operation. Further, it is assumed that medium-large organisations will have greater spending power in relation to securing their network, where the home user and SOHO users will not have as much revenue available for spending on security. Additionally, home users will be more inclined to purchase cheaper, low-end equipment as they are viewed as only wanting the service provided at the lowest cost possible, security is not high in their list of priorities when purchasing. This may be because they do not fully understand the implications of each security option or the threats which exist.

6.2 Home User Security Recommendations

The home user is viewed as having low levels of traffic and a relatively low security rating due to the nature of data traversing their networks. The data may not be as sensitive as the data travelling over a SOHO or medium to large organisational network. However, this does not mean that it should not be secured. It may be that the home user is simply using their wireless devices to enable sharing of an Internet connection, but if this is unsecured it enables unknown third parties to also share the connection as well as the IP address. This may appear harmless but it depends on what the unknown third party is using the connection for. It could be that they are using it to access or distribute illegal material or to launch Internet-based attacks using the connection and IP address as a proxy which will hide their real identity. The following recommendations, if fully implemented, should be enough to secure the home user network from unauthorised and unknown third parties and from the attacks described in the previous chapter. Below is an overview of the security measures, followed by a brief description of each method.

1   Change the default settings on the AP; the SSID and the administrator password.
2   Change the SSID regularly
3   If possible, enable MAC address-based filtering
4   If possible, disable SSID broadcasting (although some experts claim that this is not a recommended safeguard).
5   Enable WEP.

The default settings for AP hardware is information that is easily obtained. The most important element of this information is the administrator password. The administrator should be the only person who can configure or make changes to the AP's settings, and thus the network configuration and settings. If the AP's settings are left in their default state, a third party could remotely control the network using the default information widely available online.

For the home user, this may be more of an annoyance than a huge security threat, as network configuration will be minimal, with a maximum of three devices. The worst that could happen is a DoS for a short period of time until it is realised what the problem is. This is easily solved by pressing the reset button on the AP and then reconfiguring it. To avoid this type of attack it is imperative that the administrator password be changed from the default to a unique value, preferably as random a possible to include numbers as well as letters. The admin password should be changed as often as the WEP key is changed, detailed below. As demonstrated in the findings earlier, the ease with which this information can be gleaned is disturbing; however, any potential hacker may have to wait around a long time before they are lucky enough to witness a home user logging into the AP to change its configuration.

The default SSID should be changed to a unique value, and also changed often. Attackers can check the known factory set SSIDs against the network until they gain a connection; they don't require any specialised software or equipment to gain this knowledge. Changing the SSID is an extremely weak defence against attackers, there are tools which make the discovery of such information trivial, such as NetStumbler. However, changing it is better than using the default, further, it should be changed regularly so that any attackers who have gained access and come back for more will have to start the break in procedure all over again. For businesses, they should also be changed to names that are meaningless to outsiders, for example, an SSID of 'card transactions', only draws attention to information a hacker will want to get.

If possible, broadcasting the SSID should be disabled, this will depend on whether or not the hardware will allow it, some of the more low-end equipment will not allow this. SSID broadcast is where the AP constantly broadcasts its SSID as a beacon in search of stations with which to connect. By turning this feature off, stations must know the SSID in order to connect to the AP.

However, this is another relatively weak security method, the SSID will be present in other messages sent between the AP and clients, and vice versa; but, again, it is better to implement this, as every step, no matter how weak, makes the job of the attacker that bit more difficult (Moskowitz, 2003). NetStumbler will still pick up the SSID as will Ethereal.

Turning the SSID broadcast off also appears to cause some operational issues where some NICs could not re-connect to the network after the SSID broadcasting had been turned off. They simply could not sense the AP and thus could not identify an available network to connect to.

MAC address-based filtering is another option that will be hardware dependent; low-end equipment will not offer this option. This method permits access to the WLAN by certain devices according to a list of MAC addresses kept at the AP. If a device's MAC address does not appear on the list it is not permitted to associate and join the network.

However, again, this is a relatively weak method as proven in chapter four. MAC addresses can be easily spoofed, and the identity of a valid user can be stolen and used to gain access. Filtering will still make the attacker's job more difficult, so it should be implemented. Less advanced users may have problems implementing this feature as they may not understand what it is, how to implement it or how to find the MAC address of their equipment.

Enable WEP at the longest key permitted by the hardware, currently around 256-bit, and use random key sequences with little or no repeat characters. Although WEP has received much press and negative publicity, and has proven weaknesses, it is still an extremely useful security measure, especially for the home user. Devices are usually shipped with this feature turned off by default, and many home users tend not to turn it on, either because they don't know how to or they don't understand what it is.

WEP encrypts the body of each 802.11 data frame, which makes it difficult for someone with a packet analyser to decipher the actual data. (Geir, Sept 2000). For WEP to be broken a few million packets need to be captured in order to find enough with weak IVs to expose the WEP key. Airsnort is a useful tool for automating and simplifying this process. Its effectiveness was demonstrated in chapter three.

The home user is perceived as having relatively low levels of traffic, this therefore makes WEP a suitable, and strong, security measure for that group; and by ensuring that the WEP key is as long as possible (dictated by the equipment itself), WEP will deter most, if not all, potential attackers.

The home user will consequently not need to change their WEP key too often, but based on the figures in chapter three, it is recommended that it should be changed on a regular basis. At least once a month, or more, depending on the user's own assessment of their traffic load. This will avoid an attacker being able to collect enough information to break the key. If the home user is making use of their network for downloads more than three hours per day, the key should be changed more often, perhaps once every fortnight.

Because the home user would not be hugely attractive to a potential hacker, WEP would be a sufficiently strong method of protection. Traffic is typically intermittent during the day and night and an attacker would not wait around long enough to wait for enough traffic to obtain enough to break the key. After all, an attacker has not got much to gain by cracking a home network so it is unlikely that they would spend any great time and effort on this type of network.

6.3 Home Office Security recommendations

The home office has a slightly elevated security status over the purely home user, their traffic load will also be higher than that of the home user and it is assumed that it will be less intermittent and perhaps somewhat steady traffic during normal office hours, depending on the type of business being operated. 80% of the network usage is seen as being business related, with 20% being for leisure. The nature of traffic flowing over a home office network will be more sensitive than the home user's; the home office user should be aware that their business information may be open to eavesdroppers or attackers. This could in turn have a detrimental affect on the business through loss of confidentiality and integrity and through deletion or alteration of documents. In addition, attacks against the operation of the network will also affect the home office user's ability to access the network; these can range from intermittent network failure/degradation in performance, to prolonged DoS attacks.

All of the basic security recommendations aimed at the home user are equally applicable to the home office user; the home office user should implement them _all_. Implemented singly, they prove weak, but done in combination they can prove to be sufficiently strong.

In addition to all the security functions built into the equipment, the home office user should implement firewalls on all PCs, this will provide an extra layer of protection. It is recommended that the home office user should purchase equipment with a higher specification to enable them to fully implement all the security options mentioned previously and to enable 256-bit WEP keys to be used.

Although this may prove to be expensive, the cost is justified as the home user must strive to protect their business. The home office user is also viewed as having greater spending power than the home user and can therefore buy superior equipment, but they are still somewhat inhibited by cost.

The home office is at an advantage over the small office, or the medium to large organisations, because of where they are located, that is, in the home. War-divers will generally not target residential areas looking for networks to hack, they are usually more interested in more commercial or industrial networks. Therefore security implementations, as mentioned, should be enough.

Key rotation for the home office will be more frequent than the home user; keys should be changed at least once a week, again depending on traffic load, it may be required more often. This is a very feasible option for the home office as there may well only be two to three devices requiring the change, which means there is little or no key management required and the task can be carried out relatively easily.

In addition to manual key rotation, higher-end equipment that utilises TKIP functionality is a feasible option for this group of user. TKIP provides per-packet key mixing, a message integrity check and re-keying mechanism, thereby overcoming the flaws in WEP (devx.com).

6.4 Small Office Security recommendations

The small office's network traffic will be 100% business related, but will typically only have traffic during normal office hours. It can have up to 20 wireless devices, all transmitting information on the airwaves. This consequently increases the amount of network traffic, hence the amount of information available to a would-be attacker. Even if WEP is enabled, the possibility of a hacker obtaining the information they require to enable them to break a WEP key is increased and the time taken to do so. Consequently, small offices need to implement something stronger than, or in addition to, WEP and the other basic methods to secure their network and their data.

The options available to the small office are numerous, but again, the small office is more than likely to be inhibited by cost; this will subsequently narrow their choices slightly. With this in mind it is recommended that the small office should implement _all_ the basic security measures outlined previously with respect to WEP, MAC address filtering, SSIDs, passwords and firewalls. They should also strive to buy hardware with as many built in security features as possible within their spending region; low-end devices are no good.

In addition to this they should consider implementing some of the more advanced security options available. The Wi-Fi Alliance has provided SOHO users with an alternative security solution aimed specifically at that group; known as Wi-Fi Protected access, version one, Pre-Shared Key (WPA-PSK). It was derived from the upcoming 802.11i standard and addresses the vulnerabilities of WEP and adds user authentication. At this stage it is important to specify why this security option has not been recommended to the home office group. The measures already recommended, if implemented in full, should provide enough protection for the home office; it is also felt that WPA may prove difficult to understand, or perhaps too technical for the home office user, and may even be overkill.

WPA addresses the weaknesses in WEP caused by the IVs, it ensures integrity through Message Integrity Check (MIC or 'Michael') and uses Temporal Key Integrity Protocol (TKIP) to enhance data encryption (Bowman, 2003). WPA-PSK does not require the use of authentication servers, which makes it extremely suitable for use within the small office environment, where cost is an inhibitor and where the complexity of a server is uncalled for. WPA-PSK is easily introduced into an existing WLAN implementation; it is designed to be a software/firmware upgrade on devices that can support it – usually most Wi-Fi Certified products – thereby preserving investment in equipment. It is also purported to be easy to set up and run, which makes it attractive to more inexperienced users.

To set up and use WPA a password, or master key, is entered on the AP and each client device; the password allows only devices with matching passwords to join the network, it is also used to start the TKIP encryption process (Grim, 2002).

WPA-PSK strengthens encryption by automatically changing keys (dynamic re-keying) between devices after a specified period of time, or number of packets. These levels should be set in relation to network traffic levels; networks with lower traffic will have a higher threshold and vice versa (Bowman, 2003). It is recommended that the packet threshold is set to change every 500,000 packets regardless of key size. WPA-PSK is the strongest option available to this group of user; the process used to generate the encryption key is very rigorous and the re-keying is done very quickly. This prevents attackers from gathering enough data to break encryption. It significantly increases the effort required to allow passive monitoring and decryption of traffic, foiling Airsnort.

TKIP uses the same encryption algorithm as WEP, (RC4), but its dynamic nature makes it considerably more difficult for attackers to crack. TKIP fixes the flaws in WEP by creating a longer IV and increasing randomness (Dornan, 2003).

It is highly recommended that the small office user upgrade to WPA-PSK with TKIP, if the equipment allows, or if not, they should make an investment in equipment which will. It should be noted, however, that WPA is the Wi-Fi's interim answer until the IEEE's 802.11i is ratified and in use, which may not be until 2006. It is not without its problems, but it is considered strong and contains the essential elements needed for WLAN security. WPA version one is also weak when roaming is required, but this should not be a great problem in the small office environment, where one AP could probably provide coverage for the entire office. WPA version two is being designed, among other things, to overcome this short fall.

6.5 Medium to Large Organisations Security Recommendations

This group is viewed as having the highest traffic load, security rating and spending power, because of this they also have the strongest security options available to them. The following recommendations are the strongest measure available today; due to this group's security status they must implement at least one of these options in addition to, or alternative to the basic recommendations made earlier. They are large enough to justify spending on security implementations; simply on the amount of traffic that can traverse their network and the number of users.

These options are directed towards this group as they usually require dedicated IT expertise and support to administer and appropriate funding to maintain, which also makes them wholly inappropriate for any other group of user. Larger organisations with more complex WLANs with hundreds of users and APs require more sophisticated access control through incorporating RADIUS servers. It is not feasible for such large organisations to maintain huge lists of MAC addresses to implement filtering and the traffic load would be such that reliance on WEP would be futile. Indeed, on an 802.11b network operating at peek 11Mpbs speeds, a WEP key would need to be change every few hours, this would become a logistical nightmare in a network of this size. Below is an overview of the security measures recommended for this group of user, followed by a brief description of each method:

1. Wi-Fi Protected Access (WPA) for the Enterprise.
2. Virtual Private Networks (VPN)
3. Intrusion Detection Systems (IDS)
4. Documented Security Policies and Procedures

6.5.1 WPA for the Enterprise

In the 'enterprise', WPA is used in conjunction with an authentication server to provide centralised access control and management. It is scaleable and suitable for hundreds of users. Authentication can be carried out through a number of credentials, including digital certificates, unique usernames and passwords, smartcards, or other forms of secure ID. (Higgins, 2003)

WPA for the enterprise makes use of the IEEE's 802.1x infrastructure to standardise the authentication process, originally intended for wired networks. Implementing WPA for the enterprise will involve, as mentioned, an authentication server, typically RADIUS-based severs, selecting the EAP type that will be supported on all stations, APs and authentication servers, and the software upgrade of client and AP devices to enable them to use WPA (Wi-FI Alliance, February 2003). There are typically four EAP methods in use today; EAP-MD5, EAP-Cisco Wireless (LEAP), EAP-TLS and EAP-TTLS, all of which are unfortunately incompatible with each other. Refer to appendix X for details on each EAP type. It is important that organisations choose one EAP method and ensure it is applied to all equipment throughout the organisation, otherwise roaming between APs will be prohibited.

WPA enterprise provides strong security through authentication, when a device requests access to a network, the AP demands a set of credentials, the information supplied is then passed, by the AP, to a RADIUS server for authentication and authorisation (Dismukes, 2002). In addition, RADIUS allows the existence of a centralised database of user profiles which allows certain network privileges for different users, and also the power to deny participation completely; this is a very powerful network management tool.

However, because 802.1x primarily handles authentication, the data is still only as secure as its encryption makes it, therefore if WEP is used, organisations are still caught will all of its associated problems. It is recommended that TKIP at a minimum is employed for encryption, with a view to upgrading to AES in the future as part of WPA version 2, which will require new hardware. AES improves upon previous encryption methods by removing use of the RC4 algorithm and using an alternative called the Rijndael algorithm, plus longer keys of 192 and 256 in length, which makes it extremely strong. However, it requires a separate processor to avoid slowing down the network, which means that it will not be backward compatible, so a move to WPA version 2 could mean replacing all equipment in the network and is a decision that should not be taken lightly (Vaughan-Michels, 2002).

6.5.2 Virtual Private Networks (VPNs)

VPNs were originally developed to enable remote clients to securely connect to servers/networks over the public Internet, but are equally useful within the wireless environment. This may be an expensive option, but it is an alternative if not implementing WPA/802.1x. Special VPN software must be purchased and installed on each communicating device, and depending on the number of devices, this could become a huge task in its own. If the number of devices does not run into a few hundred VPN is a feasible option. In addition network administrators are advised to define a VLAN[12] which consists of all APs on the network; then configure a firewall that allows only VPN traffic to access the VLAN. Together, the firewall, VLAN and VPN ensure that wireless users are authenticated and their traffic is encrypted. This requires the skills of a dedicated network administrator, which most medium to large organisations employ (Vernier Networks, 2003). VPNs make use of the IPSec (Internet Protocol Security) protocol suite. This is a set of authentication and encryption protocols developed by IETF (Internet Engineering Task Force). It encapsulates a packet by wrapping another packet around it and then

---

[12] VLAN stands for Virtual Local Area Network. Virtual LAN's can only be specified on switch hardware allowing VLAN's to be treated as a separate logical LANs.

encrypting everything; this double-encryption forms a secure 'tunnel' across an otherwise un-secure network (McDonald, 2003).

This means wireless clients can connect securely to the organisational network through a VPN gateway on the organisational network edge. The gateway can be set up to use PSK or digital certificates; additionally user authentication to the VPN gateway can occur using RADIUS. As mentioned, VPNs can prove expensive and scale poorly. If using digital certificates, these must be purchased and tracked; VPN terminators can also become bottlenecks, depending on the level of traffic, thereby degrading network performance. VPNs would work well with a few wireless users, but if the number of users is expected to be large, VPNs are not recommended. They are better utilised for a small section of users who need mobility, but also need to be part of the wired backbone (Vernier Networks, 2003). Using VPNs to secure wireless users is recommended if new users are being added to an already established VPN infrastructure, WPA/802.1x is recommended above the use of VPNs, but if WPA/802.1x is not utilised VPN is also acceptable.

6.5.3 Intrusion Detection Systems (IDS)

This is an option that can be applied in conjunction with, or in addition to any other security measure, but should not be applied on its own. It is recommended that medium to large organisations implement these systems to monitor their network traffic to discover attempts to hack or cause a DoS. Generally speaking, there are four categories of IDS – Network Intrusion Detection Systems (NIDSes), System Integrity Verifiers (SIVs), Log File Monitoring (LFM) and Deception Systems (honeypots).

NIDSes, as the name suggests, detects attempts on the network. An example would be to watch for a large number of TCP connection requests to different ports. SIVs monitor system files in an attempt to discover when an intruder changes files, perhaps leaving behind a backdoor for later use. LFUs simply monitor log files (a file that lists actions that have occurred) and looks for patterns that would suggest an intruder is attacking (ISP-Planet). The sole purpose of a deception system is a system designed to be broken in order to lure an intruder way from more valuable systems to log and monitor their activities. Deception systems emulate the type of systems that hackers would normally target, like ftp servers, web servers, etc. This option is an extravagant one and involves the setup of an entire, false, system, purely for deceptive purposes. Many companies may not want to incur the costs of such a system, thus the use of a deception system is recommended to those organisations who feel that their data is highly sensitive enough to merit this (Schoeneck, 2003). IDSes can be further subdivided into passive and reactive systems. Passive systems detect a potential security breach, log the information and signal an alert; reactive systems respond to suspicious activity by actively logging off a user and denying them further access (Webopedia.com). It is recommended that the medium to large organisations group should implement a reactive NIDS. NIDSes detect an attempt on the network before it becomes successful, whereas SIVs and LFMs are post-event, the damage may already have been done. As mentioned, the deception system option is as an extreme measure and should only be employed if the sensitivity of the data or company operations merits it. However, it must be noted that IDSes are not foolproof, which is why they are recommended as an additional layer of security. Some intrusion attacks can go un-noticed. Environments which are especially susceptible to missed attacks are listed below; IDSes should not be utilised in these circumstances:

- *Heavy Traffic Networks*
  The high amount of traffic overloads the IDS sensor and intrusion traffic is missed. At the larger end of the medium to large organisation range, some companies may fall prey to this weakness.

- *Switch Networks*
  AN NIDS needs to see the traffic on each switch segment; in switched networks there is no ideal

location to connect an NIDS, and deploying NIDS on each segment is cost prohibitive in many environments, thereby leaving segments unprotected. If a switched network exists with many segments, perhaps an IDS should be avoided completely, or only implemented on a segment that provides access to the outside world, or on a segment that contains a system attractive to attackers, or on the segment where the wireless LAN meets the wired backbone.

- *Asymmetrical Networks*
In asymmetrical routed networks the traffic can traverse multiple paths before it reaches the NIDS which means that it will only see parts of the message flow, thereby causing it to missing an attack. An NIDS needs to see a complete conversation in order to determine if an intrusion is present. Therefore if an asymmetrical network is in use, an IDS will not be a useful option (Edwards, 2002).

6.5.4 Documented Security Policies & Procedures

Like any business function, it is important that policies and procedures for the use of WLANs are defined, mainly to protect the network, but also to protect its users. It is equally important that any policies or procedures are communicated effectively to staff; staff should be in no doubt about what they are/are not permitted to do. Clearly defined policies can protect a network from un-necessary security breaches as well as performance degradation. They are important for medium to large organisations due to the huge number of employees and devices, thus introducing an element of risk into the organisation. There is a need for centralised, management-backed, policies and procedures that are communicated to all staff. Due to its size, this group is at an increased risk of being exposed by a rogue AP; they are easy to install and provide the mobility that employees seek. Employees may think that installing a device which helps them better utilise their PC is harmless, when in reality, if they don't secure their device properly, or at all, it can become a huge security risk. It is issues like this which can be overcome by a defined and enforced security policy. AirDefense provide a 6-step guide for WLAN security and management policies, it is recommended that these guidelines are followed when implementing policies and procedures:

1. Define and Document the Policy. Ideally this should cover issues such as:

    - WLAN usage
    - Application limitations
    - Network Roaming
    - Uncontrolled environments, like public hotspots
    - Network performance issues

2. Management Support, required for enforcement
3. Educate Employees about policies
4. Monitor and Audit for Compliance
5. Enforcement if Breached
6. Revise and Fine-tune policies   (AirDefense I, 2003).

It is strongly recommended that the use of APs by employees, other than the network administration team, is completely prohibited. This should be strictly enforced as such devices can blow a huge hole in any carefully planned security measures. In addition, policies should be in place which forbid employees to alter the configuration of APs and wireless NICs, especially in relation to WEP, SSID broadcasts, etc. The AP hardware should be placed in a secure room where no one but the network administration team can gain access, this not only minimises un-necessary signal leakage, but means the hardware can be protected from reset to default by an unauthorised individual. Policies which limit transmissions to certain channels, at certain speeds and at certain times make it easier to identify an intruder operating on a different channel from the car park at a lower data rate after office hours (AirDefense II, 2003).

However, policies are useless unless a network is actively being monitored for breaches, this may be part of the network administrator's job depending on the size of the network. It is this person's responsibility to report any breaches or peculiar behaviour no matter how trivial it may appear.

7 APPENDICES

APPENDIX I: Modulation Techniques

APPENDIX II: Spread Spectrum Techniques

APPENDIX III: IEEE 802.11 standards

APPENDIX IV: The Pringles Can Antenna

APPENDIX V: Sample data from Wigle web site

APPENDIX VI: MAC Address Spoofing

APPENDIX VII: Interframe Spacing

APPENDIX VIII: Equipment used in Test WLAN

APPENDIX IX: Airsnort Install Instructions

APPENDIX X: 802.1x EAP Types

APPENDIX I: Modulation Techniques

Amplitude Modulation (AM)

To transmit information using the AM technique, the strength (amplitude) of the radio wave is altered in response to the data being mixed with it. AM is the most straightforward form of modulation, and is demonstrated graphically in Figure 15. The height of the carrier signal is changed depending on what the signal is representing at a given time (Harte, 2000).

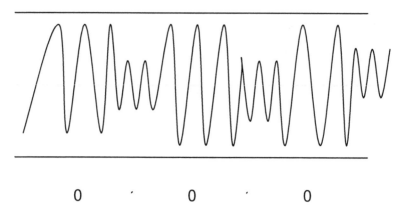

0   ·   0   ·   0

Figure 15: Amplitude Modulation

(Source: http://electronics.howstuffworks.com/radio.htm/)

Frequency Modulation (FM)

FM is more resistant to noise than AM as it uses a wider bandwidth, therefore is less susceptible to narrowband interference. Data is transferred by varying the frequency of the radio wave in relation to the date being mixed with it; the frequency of the wave differs consistently with the intensity of the data signal. See Figure 16 below for a graphical representation (FM, 2003).

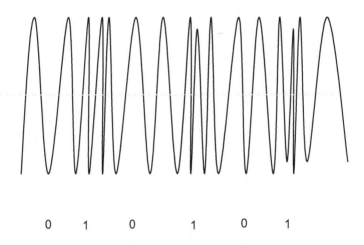

0   1   0   1   0   1

Figure 16: Frequency Modulation

(Source: http://electronics.howstuffworks.com/radio.htm/)

Phase Modulation (PM)

Information is transmitted in PM by varying the phase (or relative timing) of a radio wave in accordance with the amplitude of the data being transmitted. When the data has a negative polarity, the carrier phase shifts in one direction, and when it has a positive polarity, it shifts in the opposite direction. Figure 17 shows PM graphically (PM, 2003).

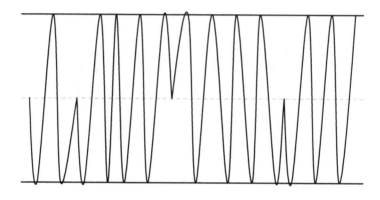

0

Figure 17: Phase Modulation

Source: http://www.ictp.trieste.it/~radionet/2001_school/lectures/fitton

APPENDIX II: Spread Spectrum Techniques

Frequency Hopping Spread Spectrum (FHSS)

Here the signal hops from frequency to frequency over a wide band of frequencies, for example, within the 2.4-2.4845 GHz range. The transmitter and receiver change the frequency they operate on in accordance with a Pseudo-Random Sequence (PRS) of numbers. To properly communicate both devices must be set to the same hopping code.

It is therefore possible to have devices, using FHSS, operate within the same frequency band and not interfere with each other, as long as they are using different hopping codes. A set of hopping codes that never use the same frequencies at the same time are considered *orthogonal* (Geier, 1999).

Direct Sequence Spread Spectrum (DSSS)

DSSS combines a data signal with a higher data rate bit sequence, referred to as a 'chipping code'. The data is exclusive ORed (XOR) with a PRS which results in a higher bit rate, this increases the signal's resistance to interference.

Chipping Code: 0 = 11101100011
                       1 = 00010011100

Data Stream: 1 0 1

Transmitted Sequence:

1	0	1
00010011100	11101100011	00010011100

Figure 18: Chipping Code (Geier, 1999)

Figure 18 shows an example of how DSSS works. A chipping code is assigned to represent the logic 1 and logic 0 data bits. When the data stream is transmitted, the code is what is sent

APPENDIX III: IEEE 802.11 STANDARDS

The 802.11 specification has three transmission options; one infrared (IR) option, and two radio frequency options; FHSS and DSSS. IR is outside the scope of this book and therefore will not be covered. IEEE have developed several specifications for WLAN technology, the names of which resemble the alphabet. There are basically two categories of standards; those that specify the fundamental protocols for the complete wireless system, these are called 802.11a, 802.11b and 802.11g; and those that address specific weaknesses or provide additional functionality, these are 802.11d, e, f, h, I, j, k, m and n (3Com Corporation, 2003).

The three fundamental standards are listed first, followed by an alphabetical style listing of the extensions as opposed to chronological order, to provide ease of reading and division.

802.11 – The Original

This is formally known as the 'IEEE Standard for Wireless LAN Medium Access Control (MAC) and Physical Layer (PHY) specifications'. The scope of this project was to develop MAC and PHY specifications for wireless connectivity, within the 2.4GHz band. The MAC is designed to support PHY layer units, as mentioned; it contains two radio units and one infrared. This original standard only specified data rates of 1 and 2 Mbps. This was in 1997. In 1999, two more elements, 802.11a and 802.11b were added with the specific aim of achieving higher bandwidths. These two elements use very different methods to do this,as will become evident (IEEE standards Status Report).

802.11a

Although 802.11a is being covered first, it was not the first extension, this was 802.11b. 802.11a is an extension of the original standard that operates in the

5GHz range with a throughput of 54Mpbs and a range of 50-60 feet. It provides up to 12 channels for communications using an advance radio technique called Orthogonal Frequency Division Multiplexing (OFDM) Instead of sending data bits sequentially at a very high data rate, OFDM sends multiple data streams in parallel over separate radio carrier signals (Computer Associates, 2003). An advantage of 802.11a is that it operates in the relatively un-congested 5GHz band, which has more than three times the available spectrum than the 2.4GHz band. However, the range is much shorter than 802.11b, and multiple 802.11a APs are required to cover the same range provided by an 802.11b AP, roughly four times as much - which can prove to be expensive to implement.

Another important drawback is that because 802.11a and 802.11b employ different radio bands, 802.11a is not backward compatible with the more popular 802.11b, and with 802.11b so widely entrenched the cost of initial 802.11a deployments may be difficult to justify. Although dual cards will become available, they will cost more. Due to this 802.11a may not become as mainstream as 802.11b, or dropped completely in favour of the equally speedy 802.11g, which operates at 54Mpbs, and is backward compatible with 802.11b (Geier, 2002).

802.11b

As mentioned, 802.11b was developed and available before 802.11a, which is probably why it has such a strong foot-hold in the wireless market, it was the first extension to the original 802.11 standard. 802.11b practically launched the industry as the market overwhelmingly accepted it. This specification operates at 2.4GHz frequency with a throughput of 11Mbps and a range of 200-300 feet. Where 802.11a operates of 12 channels, 802.11b only offers 3 for communications using DSSS or FHSS. 802.11b allows wireless functionality comparable to wired Ethernet, also referred to as High

Rate or Wi-Fi[13] (Computer Associates, 2003). 802.11b is the most commonly implemented wireless networking communications standard, with the largest number of vendor implementations available, and costs roughly a quarter as much as an 802.11a network, covering the same area at the same data rate, this is its main advantage. However, a downside is that 802.11b operates in the increasingly congested 2.4GHz radio band, also used by Bluetooth, cordless phones and even microwave ovens. This may serve to reduce the data rate due to issues with interference; this would be the main disadvantage, as far as cost is concerned (3Com Corporation, 2003). The widespread use of 802.11b has, however, exposed some shocking security weaknesses, and keeping track of these developments and designing a network appropriately can become a task in its own. This is the main reason for all the extensions and revisions to the standard.

802.11g

This specification operates in the 2.4GHz frequency range with a throughput of 5Mpbs at a range of 100-200 feet. A major issue that makes moving to 802.11g more attractive is its backward compatibility with 802.11b, and it offers speeds similar to those of 802.11a. This may be the end of the adoption of 802.11a. It may immediately be a winner by preserving investment in 802.11b equipment, whilst also moving speeds forward (Computer Associates, 2003). 802.11g adopts 802.11a's OFDM method to obtain speeds of 54Mbps, however, like 802.11b, 802.11g handles only three channels. This means that same problems with channel assignment will be encountered when covering a large area where there is a high density of users. Another shared problem between 'b' and 'g' is the issue of radio frequency interference from other devices within the 2.4GHz band (Geier, 2002).

The following few paragraphs are the extensions (except 'h' and 'j') that apply to all three of the above variants of 802.11.

---

[13] The term Wi-Fi is used by the Wireless Ethernet Compatibility Alliance to specify products that conform to the 802.11b standard.

802.11c

This is a little known, or talked about, extension. The official purpose of 802.11c is cited as:

"to provide the required 802.11 specific information to the IS 10038 (802.1D) standard'.

In fact the writer found it difficult to obtain information on this little known extension, other than what is provided by the IEEE organisation. It's a modified 802.1D – MAC Level Bridging – to include 802.11 frames, thus helping with quality of service and filtering issues. It is a useful standard of no interest to anyone, except those who are designing WLAN hardware. It is basically a standard to improve interoperability between devices (IEEE Standards Status Report).

802.11d

Next, the relatively more popular 802.11d standard. This addresses regulatory considerations in countries that do not yet have rules in place for the operation of 802.11 LANs. 802.11d ensures interoperability of WLANs in those countries. Basically, this is a global harmonising group; different countries have different parts of the 2.4 and 5 GHz bands available for unlicensed networking. 802.11d seeks to help create standards that will be approvable in as many different countries as possible (3Com Corporation, 2003). The IEEE states this supplement will define the physical layer requirements to extend the operation of 802.11 WLANs into new domains. That is, the definition of channelization, hopping patterns, etc. It will allow equipment to operate in markets not served by the current standards (IEEE Standards Status Report).

802.11e

This is an important extension that adds Quality-of-Service (QoS) features and multimedia support to the existing 802.11b and 802.11a wireless standards, while maintaining full backward compatibility with those standards. It is a MAC level initiative, which in brief, allows packets with specific requirements for transmission delay and bandwidth to be passed preferentially to those with laxer needs. This will let, time sensitive, streamed audio and video work better (Parks, 2001). The original 802.11 MAC control protocol was designed with two modes of communication for wireless stations. The first is Distributed Coordination Function (DCF); which provides coordination, but it does not support any type of priority access to the medium. The second, optional mode, is Point Coordination Function (PCF); which supports time-sensitive traffic. However, PCF hasn't been broadly adopted because the technology's transmission times are unpredictable.

Because DCF and PCF do not differentiate between traffic types or sources, the IEEE are proposing enhancements in 802.11e to both coordination modes to facilitate QoS. The proposed enhancements introduce the concept of traffic categories into DCF; where each station has eight traffic categories, or priority levels. This enhancement is called Enhanced DCF or EDCF. Using EDCF, stations try to send data after detecting the medium is idle and after waiting a period of time defined by the corresponding interframe space (see appendix VII for details on interframe spacing). A higher priority traffic category will have a shorter interframe space than a lower priority one, thus meaning stations with lower-priority traffic must wait longer than those with high-priority traffic before trying to access the medium (Thomas, 2003). 802.11e extends the polling mechanism of PCF with the Hybrid Coordination Function (HCF). A hybrid controller polls stations during a contention-free period, the polling grants a station a specific start time and a maximum transmit duration, thereby controlling and managing access to the medium.

802.11f

802.11f is one of the lesser known standards in the IEEE 802.11 family; 802.11f describes communications between APs of differing vendors in one system, more specifically, the roaming of users between these different devices and how user information is past between the APs (also known as 'hand-off'). The Inter-Access Point Protocol (IAPP), handles the registration of APs within a network and the exchange of information when a user is roaming among coverage areas supported by different vendor's APs. It aims to increase interoperability between differing APs (NWFusion Encyclopedia). The original standard did not specify the communications between APs in order to provide some flexibility in working with different distribution systems (i.e., wired backbones that interconnect APs). Consequently, AP vendors then implemented their own versions of the hand-off between their devices, meaning that APs from different vendors will not always deal with hand-off smoothly, if at all.

802.11h

The 'h' is for HiperLAN – a European standard for wireless LANs. 802.11h adds features to 802.11a to make it suitable for European use and be HiperLAN. These features are frequency and power management to make sure that 802.11a networks don't interfere with radar and satellite services in Europe. 802.11a and 802.11h both operate in the 5GHz band, and are nearly identical, except that 802.11h adds Transmit Power Control (TPC) which limits the wireless network card from emitting more radio signal than is needed, and Dynamic Frequency Selection (DFS), which lets the device listen to what is happening in the airspace before picking a channel. TPS and DFS are required features in Europe (Computer Associates, 2003).

802.11i

802.11i is a major extension because it was intended to improve WLAN security on 802.11a and 802.11b networks, which was in tatters. It adds two main blocks of improvements; improved security for data in transit, and better control of who can use a network. It covers key management and distribution, encryption and authentication, the three main components of security (Goodwins, 2003). The 802.11i specification can be viewed as consisting of three main sections, organised into two layers. On the lower level are improved encryption algorithms in the form of the Temporal Key Integrity Protocol (TKIP) and the counter mode with Cipher Block Chaining-Message Authentication Code, CBC-MAC protocol (CCMP). Both of these provide enhanced data integrity over WEP, with TKIP being targeted at legacy equipment and CCMP being targeted at future WLAN equipment. Above TKIP and CCMP sits 802.1x, a standard for port based access control developed by a different body within the IEE 802 organisation. As used in 802.11i, 802.1x provides a framework for robust user authentication and encryption key distribution, both features originally missing from the 802.11 standard (Eaton, 2002).

TKIP introduces a sophisticated key generation function which encrypts every data packet with its own unique encryption key. This increases the complexity of decoding the keys by reducing the amount of data available to a hacker that has been encrypted using a particular key. The mixing function takes the base WEP key, the transmitter's MAC address and the packet sequence number as inputs; this is then mixed with an Initialisation Vector (IV) and run through the RC4 algorithm, which generates one unique key per packet. This is supposed to counteract the attacks based on the weaknesses in the key scheduling algorithm of RC4, famously identified by Flurer, Martin and Shamir (Phifer, 2002). In addition to TKIP encryption, 802.11i defines a new encryption method based on the Advanced Encryption Standard (AES). AES based encryption can be used in a number of different modes or algorithms. The mode that has been chosen for 802.11i is the counter mode with CBC-MAC. The counter mode delivers data privacy while the CBC-MAC delivers data integrity and authentication (Eaton, 2002). Ultimately IEEE is expected to use the AES, however, AES requires considerably more computing power than most existing 802.11b cards can provide. Keeping RC4 for now means that TKIP can be deployed in firmware upgrades instead of new chipsets, thereby protecting investment in 802.11 equipment (Phifer, 2002). 802.1x does not define any encryption standards, instead it handles authentication and key management.

It can be used with any cipher and with many authentication methods. It takes advantage of an existing authentication protocol know as Extensible Authentication Protocol (EAP). EAP messages are encapsulated in an 802.1x message and referred to as EAPOL, or EAP over LAN (Roshan, 2001). 802.1x communications begin with an unaunthenticated client device attempting to connect with an AP. The AP responds by allowing the client device to pass only EAP packets to an authentication server (usually a RADIUS[14] server), located on the wired side of the AP. The AP blocks all other traffic types until the AP can verify the client's identity using the authentication server. Once authenticated, the client is permitted to pass other types of traffic, such as HTTP, POP3, etc (Geier, May 2002).

802.1x also specifies how keys are passed back to the client to be used in further network traffic – how keys are used is not specified, but how they are transferred securely is. It also sets a per-packet authentication key that can't be faked by a third party, maintaining authentication if the client roams to another port and preventing interception and taking over a session by an intruder (Goodwins, 2002).

802.11j

This is the Japanese version of 802.11a. Like 802.11h, 802.11j adjusts 802.11a to work in the 4.9-5GHz frequency assigned to high-speed WLANs in Japan, to conform to the Japanese rules an operational mode, operational rate, radiated power, emissions and channel sense (IEEE P802).

802.11k

This project aims to standardise the way 802.11a, b and g report measurement of radio and network conditions to

---

[14] Remote Authentication Dial-in User Service)

other parts of the network protocol stack and new applications. It is called Radio Resource Management. The standard focuses on two key WLAN elements: APs and PC cards (NICs). The goal is to make measurements from layers one and two of the OSI protocol stack - physical and data link layers – available to the upper layers. It is expected that the upper layers will then be able to make decisions about the radio environment.

One feature is better traffic distribution. Normally a wireless device will connect to whatever AP gives it the strongest signal. However, this can lead to an overload on some APs and under-load on others, resulting in an overall lowered service level. The 802.11k standard will allow network management software to detect this situation and redirect some of the users to under-utilised APs. Although those APs may have weaker signals, they are able to provide greater throughput, this will provide higher speeds for both those on the original AP and those that were redirected (Robb, 2003).

802.11L

802.11 'l' was never used as the 'l' can be easily confused with other letters of the alphabet, i.e., 'i'.

802.11m

This extension is a maintenance update to 802.11 (hence the 'm') that will roll-up changes made to 80-11-99, y 802.11a,b and d, etc., into the 2003 revision of the 802.11 standard. Periodically all amendment standards are rolled-up into one document. A maintenance group comes along and goes through it all democratically, hence the formation of the 802.11m working group. This standard is basically a collection of maintenance releases for 802.11 as a whole, internal IEEE housekeeping (Griffith, 2003).

802.11n

This is the last, for now, extension in the long line of letters of 802.11 extensions. 802.11n is a relatively new addition, called the High Throughput Group. They are working on a potential high-performance standard that would boost both 802.11b and 802.11a 11Mbps and 54Mbps, respectively. Proposals say it could go to 108Mbps or beyond, to as much as 320Mpbs. This standard is not expected to be complete until 2005 or 2006. Not much else has been written about 802.11n yet (Wi-Fi Planet Staff, 2003). To summarise all the 802.11 working groups, standards and extensions, Table 3 has been provided to give an 'at-a-glance' overview.

802.11 letter suffice	What it does	Status
A	55Mbps in the 5GHz band	Finished
B	11Mbps in the 2.4GHz band	Finished
C	MAC Level Bridging	Finished
D	Global harmonizing	Ongoing
E	QoS for MAC level issues	Ongoing
F	Inter-AP roaming Protocol	Ongoing
G	Increases data rate to 54Mbps in 2.4GHz	Ongoing
H	Adds dynamic frequency selection to 802.11a to comply with European regulations	Ongoing
I	Security Upgrade	Ongoing
J	A version of 802.11a for Japan	Ongoing
K	Radio resources management	Ongoing
L	Not used as confusing	_____
M	Maintenance releases	Ongoing
N	High-Throughput	Ongoing
O	Not used as confusing	_____

Table 3: IEEE 802.11 Standards & Extensions

Source: (Leira, 2003)

APPENDIX IV: THE PRINGLES CAN ANTENNA

The instructions for this Pringles can antenna have been taken in entirety from the excellent 'Building Wireless Community Networks' book by Flickenger (Flickenger, 2002).

Parts List:

1. All-thread, 5 5/8" long, 1/8" OD
2. Two nylon lock nuts
3. Five 1" washers, 1/8" ID
4. 6" aluminium tubing, ¼" ID
5. A connector to match your radio pigtail (perhaps a good female N connector)
6. 1 ½" piece of 12-gauge solid copper wire
7. A tall Pringles can (any flavour, Ridges optional)
8. Scrap plastic disc, 3" across (like another Pringles can lid)

Tools:

1. Ruler
2. Scissors
3. Pipe Cutter (hacksaw or dremel)
4. Heavy duty cutters (to cut all thread)
5. Something sharp to pierce the plastic (an awl or drill bit)
6. Hot glue gun
7. Soldering Iron

Mark and cut four pieces of tubing, about 1.2". Cut the all-thread to exactly 5 5/8". Pierce a hole in the centre of the Pringles can lid big enough for the all-thread to pass through. Cut a 3" plastic disc, just big enough to fit snugly inside the can. Another Pringles lid with the outer ridge trimmed off can do the trick. Poke a hole in the centre of it, and slip it over one of the lengths of pipe.

Now, assemble the pipe. You might have to use a file or dremel tool to shave the tips of the thread, if you have trouble getting the nuts on. The pipe is a sandwich that goes on the all-thread like this:

Nut Lid Washer Pipe Washer Pipe Washer Pipe-with-Plastic Washer Pipe Washer Nut

Tighten down the nuts to be snug, but don't over-tighten (aluminium bends quite easily), this is now the front collector. Now the can.

Wipe out the can, and measure 3 3/8" up from the bottom of the can. Cut a hole just big enough for the connector to pass through. On the Pringles Salt and Vinegar can, the N connector was directly between *Sodium* and *Protein*.

Straighten the heavy copper wire, and solder it to the connector. When inside the can, the wire should be just below the midpoint of the can (around 1 1/16"). You lose a few db by going longer, so cut it just shy of the middle of the can. Use the glue to hold the connector in place.

Now, insert the collector assembly into the can, and close the lid. The inside end of the pipe should NOT touch the copper element; it should be just forward of it. If it touches, your all-thread is probably too long.

Now, connect your pigtail, aim carefully, and you're off!

Over a clear line of sight, with short antenna cable, a 12db to 12db can-to-can shot should be able to carry an 11Mbps link well over ten miles.

(Taken from 'Building Wireless Networks' Flickenger, 2003)

APPENDIX V: SAMPLE INFORMATION FROM WIGLE.NET WEB SITE

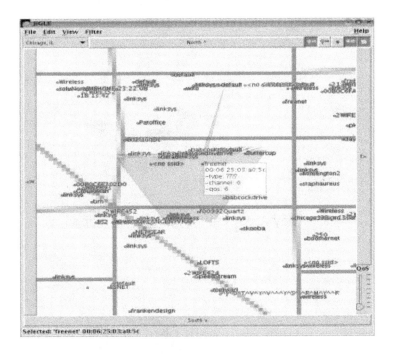

JiGLE: Chicago zoomed in, with station labels and area
plotting on, and a station selected

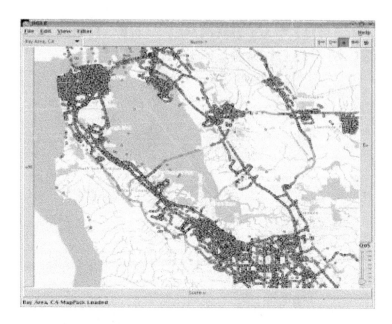

JiGLE: Bay Area, California (<u>special mappack</u>)

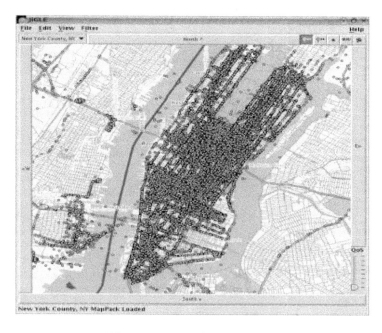

JiGLE: New York, New York

JiGLE: Chicago aerial image created by mentat's script

All screenshots are taken from the Wigle.net web site at
http://www.wigle.net.

APPENDIX VI: MAC ADDRESS SPOOFING

This is dependant on the type of NIC you have.

a) Go to Start>Settings>Control Panel and double click on Network and Dial-up Connections.

b) Right click on the NIC you want to change the MAC address and click on properties.

c) Under the "General" tab, click on the "Configure" button.

d) Click on the "Advanced" tab.

e) Under "Property section", you should see an item called "Network Address" or "Locally Administered Address", click on this.

f) On the right side, under "Value", type in the New MAC address you want to assign to your NIC. Usually this value is entered without the "-" between the MAC address numbers.

g) Goto command prompt and type in "ipcongi/all" or "net config rdr" to verify the changes.

h) If successful, reboot your system.

Please note that "00-00-00-00-00-00" if NOT a valid MAC address. Alternatively you can download the SMAC utility from the page: http://www.klcconsulting.net/smac/

These instructions have been taken in their entirety from http://www.klcconsulting.net/Change_MAC_w2k.htm

APPENDIX VII: INTERFRAME SPACING

After a frame has been transmitted, some dead time is required before any station may send. This known as Interframe spacing, which contains four intervals, is illustrated in Figure 19 below:

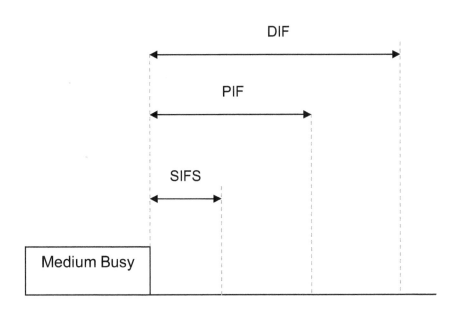

Figure 19: Interframe Spacing

These spacing intervals defer a station's access to the medium and provide various levels of priority. Each interval defines the time from the end of the last symbol of the previous frame to the beginning of the first symbol of the next frame.

Shortest Interframe Space (SIFS)

SIFS is the shortest of the interframe spaces, providing the highest priority level by allowing some frames to access the medium before others. The following frames use the SIFS interval; ACK and CTS, as these frame types require expedient access to the network to minimise retransmissions.

PCF-**IFS** (**PIFS**)

The PIFS is the interval that stations operating under the PCF mode use to gain access to the medium. This provides priority over frames sent under the DCF mode.

DCD-**IFS** (**DIFS**)

All stations operating according to DCF use the DIFS interval for transmitting data and management frames. This spacing interval makes transmission of these frames lower priority than PCF-based transmissions.

APPENDIX VIII : EQUIPMENT USED IN BOOK

1. Toshiba Satellite 1110 notebook computer, Windows XP
2. Hewlett Packard Omnibook XE3i notebook computer, Windows XP
3. Hewlett Packard Pavilion zt1141s notebook computer, Windows XP and Linux Mandrake 9.1
4. Buffalo Airstation 802.11b PCMCIA NIC, model WLI-PCM-L11GP, with external antenna connector
5. Adaptec Ultra Wireless for Notebooks 802.11b PCMCIA NIC, model AWN-8030, with Prism II chipset
6. D-Link Air 802.11b PCMCIA NIC, model DWL-610
7. Linksys 802.11b Access Point, model WAP11
8. 5dbi magnetic base external antenna
9. Pigtails for connection between antenna and NIC
10. Garmin GPS Device and serial to USB cable

APPENDIX IX: AIRSNORT INSTALL GUIDE

This installation procedure is based on the use of an Adaptec Ultra Wirless PCMCIA network card for Notebooks, model AWN-8030. This is a prism II-based card.

1. Using Mandrake control centre (bottom left of task bar, last icon on right), Software management, RpmDrake helps you install software packages, install the following packages (Use the search option to locate and then click to install in lower left window):

    a. Kernel-source-2.4.21-0.13mdk
    b. Pcmcia-cs-3.2.3-5mdk
    c. Pcmcia-cs-x11-3.2.3-5mdk
    d. Wireless-tools-25-4mdk
    e. libglib1.2-develop-1.2.10-6mdk
    f. libglib2.0_0-devel-2.2.1-1mdk
    g. libpcap0-0.7.2-1mdk
    h. flex-2.5.4a-20mdk
    i. libiw25-25-4mdk
    j. libiw25-develop-25-4mdk
    k. libgnomeui2-2.2.0.1mdk
    l. libgnomeui2_0-2.2.-.1-2mdk
    m. libgnomeui2_0-devel-2.2.0.1-2mdk

2. Using file manager – super user mode (K start button, applications, file tools)

    a. Goto location: file:/mnt/
    b. Then go to removable and select FD
    c. open file linux-wlan-ng-0.2.1-pre11.tar.gz
    d. copy file linux-wlan-ng-0.2.1-pre11
    e. Goto location file:/usr/src
    f. Paste
    g. Close down file manager

3. Using Konsole – supetr User Mode (K start button, terminals)

  a. Change down into directory "cd /usr/src/linux-wlan-ng-0.2.1-pre11"
  b. Enter "make config"
  c. Select Y to build PCMCIA
  d. N for PCI
  e. N for USB
  f. N for USB
  g. Just press enter on rest of options
  h. Type "make all"
  i. Type "make install"

4. type "kedit /etc/sysconfig/pcmcia"

  a. Change PCMCIA=no to PCMCIA=yes
  b. Add or alter line starting PCIC to be PCIC="i82375"
  c. Alt f s, alt f q

5. type "kedit /etc/pcmcia/config"

  a. Search for wireless lan section (edit, find, "wireless")
  b. Enter code for Adaptec card below the last # comment
  c. Code is as follows:

    Card "Adaptec Wireless PC Card V3.0"
      manfid 0x9005, 0x0021
      bind "Orinoco_cs"
  d. Alt f s, alt f q

6. type in "/etc/rc.d/init.d/pcmcia restart"

7. Using file manager – super user mode (K start button, applications, file tools)

  a. Goto location: file:/mnt/
  b. Then go to removable and select FD
  c. copy file Airsnort-0.2.1b-1mdk.i586.rpm
  d. Goto location file:/tmp

e. Paste

f. Close down file manager

8. Using Konsole – supetr User Mode (K start button, terminals)

    a. Change down into directory "cd /tmp"

    b. Enter "rpm i- Airsnort-0.2.1b-1mdk.i586.rpm"

9. Insert Adaptec card

10. Type in "airsnort"

APPENDIX X : 802.1X EAP TYPES

EAP-MD5

This is the earliest EAP type and relies on an MD5 hash of a username and password to pass credentials to the RADIUS server. It is a one-way authentication of client to network using passwords, therefore the network is not authenticated. This opens it up to a MITM style attack or rogue AP attack. Because of its security vulnerabilities, its use is not recommended for security-conscious enterprises (Snyder, 2002).

LEAP

This is a Cisco proprietary protocol, developed by them in conjunction with the 802.1x standard. When LEAP authenticates a user, one time WEP keys are dynamically generated for that session. LEAP also stipulates mutual authentication, which overcomes the two attacks mentioned above. However, there is one security drawback and one operational drawback; LEAP uses a weak version of MS-CHAP (version 1) to pass the login credentials for the client and AP, it has know vulnerabilities and a determined enough hacker with the right tools can compromise security (dictionary attacks). LEAP currently only works well on Cisco end-to-end networks, which will cause interoperability problems with multi-vendor equipment (Funk Software).

EAP-TLS

Developed by Microsoft and is the security method used in the 802.1x client in Windows XP. It utilises certificates to handle authentication, for the client and server sides. Like LEAP, EAP-TLS offers dynamic one-time WEP key generation and provides mutual authentication. However, the first hindrance to implementing EAP-TLS is in the burden of Public Key Infrastructure (PKI). If an organisation does not already have a PKI in place handing our certificates to trusted parties, there is a potentially steep learning curve associated with its implementation; there is also confusion on how certificates are handed out (Snyder, 2002).

EAP-TTLS

If organisations don't want to issue certificates to all wireless users, EAP-TTLS is an option for authentication. EAP-TTLS was developed jointly by Funk Software and Certicom. The AP still identifies itself to the client with a server certificate, but the user now sends their credentials in username/password form. EAP-TTLS is reportedly easy to setup and manage, eliminating the need to configure certificates for each WLAN client The only challenge to EAP-TTLS is that its slightly less secure than the dual-certificate approach of EAP-TLS, and interoperability issues due to Funk and Meetinhouse products support only; it is currently only a proposal with the IEEE at present (Dismukes).

8 REFERENCES

3Com Corporation, 'Deploying 802.11 Wireless LANs', 2003,http://www.3com.com/other/pdfs/products/en_US/wireless_lans_wp.pdf

AirDefense, 'Wireless LAN Security – What Hackers Know That You Don't' http://ssl.salesforce.com/servlet.Email/AttachmentDownload?q=00m0000000003Pr00D00000000hiyd00500000005k8d5, article is undated, but the copyright is 2003, article e-mailled by one of AirDefense's staff, accessed 18th August 2003.

AirDefense I, 'Wireless LAN Policies for Security Management', White Paper, http://ssl.salesforce.com/servlet/servlet/EmailAttachmentDownload?q=00m0000000005ak00d00000000hiyd00500000005k8d5, report undated, but copyrighted 2003, date accessed 28th January 2004.

AirDefense II, '5 Practical Steps to Secure your WLAN', http://ssl.salesforce.com/servlet/servlet.EmailAttachnmentDownload?q=00m0000000005af00d0000000hiyd0050000005k8d5, report undated, but copyrighted in 2003, date accessed 28th January 2004.

AirSnort FAQ, 'How the crack process works', http://airsnort.shmoo.com/faq.html, article undated, date accessed, 25th October 2003.

BBC News, 'Welcome to the era of drive-by hacking', http://news.bbc.co.uk/1/hi/sci/tech/1639661.stm, article date 6th November 2001, date accessed 29th October 2003.

Bellardo, John, Savage, Stefan, '802.11 Denial of Service Attacks: Real Vulnerabilities and Practical Solutions', http://www.cs.ucsd.edu/users/savage/papers/UsenixSec03.pdf, article undated, date accessed 5th November 2003.

Borisov, Nikita, Goldberg, Ian and Wagner, David, 'Security of the WEP algorithm, http://www.isaac.cs.berkeley.edu/isaac/wep-faq.html, article undated, date accessed 6th November 2003.

Borisov, Nikita, Goldber, Ian and Wager, David, 'Intercepting Mobile Communications: The Insecurity of 802.11', http://www.isaac.cs.berkely.edu/isaac/ewp-draft.pdf, article undated, date accessed 7th November 2003.

Bowman, Barb, 'WPA Wireless Security for Home Networks',http://www.microsoft.com/WindowsXP/expertz one/columns/bowman/03july28.asp, article dated 28th July 2003, date accessed 15th December 2003.

Broersma, Matthew, 'Britain Hottest in Europe for Wi-Fi', http://new.zdnet.co.uk/print/?TYPE=story&AT=39020348 t-100000015c, article date 13th August 2003, accessed 12th September 2003.

Cam-Winget, Nancy, Walker, Atheros Jesse, Aboda, Bernard and Kubler, Joe, 'Rapid Re-Keying WEP a recommended practice to improve WLAN Security', http://www.drizzle.com/~aboda/IEEE/wepimprovF.ppt, PowerPoint presentation, dated August 2001, date accessed 18th November 2003.

Computer Associates, 'Who's Watching Your Wireless Network?',http://wp.bitpipe.com/resource/org_94319714 9_209/wireless_network_wp_bpx.pdf, report dated 10th February 2003, downloaded on 27th September 2003.

Descoeudres, Oliver, 'Wireless: Wide Open to Attack', http://techupdate.zdnet.com/techupdate/stories/main/0,1 4179,2895306,00.html, article dated 22nd October 2002, date accessed 29th October 2003.

Dismukes, Trey "Azariah", 'Wireless Security Blackpaper', http://arstechnica.com/paedia/w/wireless/security-1.html, article last revised 18th July 2002, date accessed 18th September 2003.

Dornan, Andy, 'Wireless Security: Is Protected Access Enough?',http://www.ncasia.com/ViewArt.cfm?Magid=3& Artid=21977&Catid=4&subcat=48, article dated 3rd November 2003, date accessed 20th November 2003. Devx.com, 'Temporal Key Integrity Protocol (TKIP)', http://www.devx.com/wireless/Door/11455, definition, not dated, date accessed 14th January 2004

Edwards, Simon, 'Network Intrusion Detection Systems: Important IDS Network Security Vulnerabilities', http://www.forumintrusion.com/archive/IDSB_White_Pap era141002.pdf, article dated September 2002, date accessed 20th November 2003.

Eaton, Dennis, 'Diving into the 802.11i Spec: A Tutorial', http://www.commsdesign.com/printableArticle?doc_id=O EG20021126S0003, article dated 26th November 2002, date accessed 26th October 2003.

Farrow, Rik, 'VPN Vulnerabilities, VPNs might be tunnelling more through your firewall than you'd like', http://www.networkmagazine.com/article/NMG20020603 S0004, article dated 5th June 2002, date accessed 12th November 2003.

Fleishman, Glen, 'Weak Defense...But Getting Better', http://wifinetnews.com/archives/001034.html, article dated 13th March 2003, date accessed 18th November 2003.

Flickenger, Rob, 'Building Wireless Community Networks', O'Reilly & Associates Inc, 2002, California, USA.

(FM), Frequency Modulation, http://its.bldrdoc.gov/fs-1037/dir-016/_2377.htm, accessed on 18th October 2003.

Franklin, Curtis, 'A Cracked Spec', http://www.internetweek.com/reviews01/rev031201-2.htm, article dated 12th March 2001, date accessed 7th November 2003.

Funk Software, 'Security Authentication, Access Control, and Data Privacy on Wireless LANs', http://www.funk.com/radius/Solns/wlan_ody_wo.asp, article undated, date accessed 31st October 2003.

Geier, Jim, 'Making the Choice: 802.11a or 802.11g', http://www.wi-iplanet.com/tutorials/article.php/1009431, article dated 15th April 2002, accessed on 23rd October 2003.

Geier, Jim, '802.1x Offers Authentication and Key Management', http://www.wi-fiplanet.com/tutorials/article.php/1041171, article dated 7th May 2002, date accessed 23rd October 2003.

Geier, Jim, 'Wireless LANs, Implementing Interoperable Networks', MacMillan Network Architecture and Development Series, 1999, MacMillan Technical Publishing, USA.

Geier, Jim, 'Guarding Against WLAN Security Threats', http://www.wi-iplanet.com/tutorials/article.php/1462031, article dated 12th September 2000, date accessed 18th November 2003.

Goodwins, Rupert, '802.11i – designed to integrate', http://www.zdnet.co.uk/print/?TYPE=story&AT=2133239-39020430t-20000015c, article dated 10th April 2003, accessed 23rd October 2003.

Griffith, Eric, '802.11g Approved by IEEE Working Group', http://wi-fiplanet.com/news/article.php/1584761, article date 14th February 2003, date accessed 23rd October 2003.

Griffth, Eric, "Mapping the Lack of Security', http://www.wi-fiplanet.com/news/article.php/1488541, article dated 25th October 2002, date accessed 19th September 2003.

Grimm, Brian, 'Overview, Wi-Fi Protected Access', http://www.weca.net/OpenSection/pdf/Wi-Fi_Protected_Access_Overview.pdf, article dated 31st October 2003, date accessed 15th December 2003.

Harte, Lawrence, Kellog, Steven, Dreher, Richard and Schaffinit, Tom, 'The Comprehensive Guide to Wireless Technologies: Cellular, PCS, Paging, SMR and Satellite', APDG Publishing, 2000, NC USA.

Higgins, Tim, 'Wi-Fi Protected Access (WPA) need to know – part II', http://www.smallnetbuilder.com/sections-article50-page11.php, article dated 25th June 2003, date accessed 11th February 2004.

IEEE Standards Status Report, http://standards.ieee.org/cgi-bin/status, accessed 22nd September 2003

IEEE P802 – Task Group J Status, http://grouper.ieee.org/groups/802/11/Reports/tgj_update.htm, date accessed 23rd October 2003.

iLabs, Wireless Security Team, 'What's Wrong with WEP?', http://www.nwfusion.com/research/2002/0909wepprimer.html, article dated 9th September 2002, date accessed 23rd October 2003.

Information Technology E-Business Group, 'VPN and WEP, Wireless 802.11b security in a corporate environment', Intel IT White Paper, http://www.intel.com/business/bss/infrastructure/security/vpn_wep.pdf, January 2003, dated accessed 19th September 2003.

ISP-Planet, 'Intrusion Detection Systems Directory', http://www.isp-planet.com/services/ids/, article undated, date accessed 21st November 2003.

IT Glossary, 'Passive Attack', http://www.itglossary.net/passiveatt.html, definition undated, date accessed 23rd October 2003.

Jacques, Robert, 'Wi-Fi turns us into busy worker bees', http://www.theregister.co.uk/content/69/33977.html, dated 13th November 2003, accessed 27th November 2003.

Karygiannis, Tom and Owens, Les, National Institute of Standards and Technology, Special Publication 800-48, Draft, http://csrc.nist.gov/publications/drafts/draft-sp800-48.pdf, report undated, date accessed 18th August 2003.

Leira, Jardar, 'Status of the IEEE 802.11 Standards', http://www.uninett.no/wlan/ieee80211x.html, article dated 1st March 2003, date accessed 23rd October 2003.

McClure, Stuart, Scambray, Joel and Jurtz, George, 'Hacking Exposed: Network Security Secrets and Solutions', 4th Edition, Osbourne McGraw-Hill, 2003.

McDonald, Christopher, 'Virtual Private Networks', http://www.intranetjournal.com/text/foundation/vpn-2.shtml, article undated, but copyrighted 2002, date accessed 20th November 2003.

Me, Gianluigi, 'A threat posed by SNMP use over WLAN', http://www.wi-fitechnology.com/Wi-Fi_Reports_and_Papers/SNMP_use_over_WLAN.html, article dated 5th October 2003, date accessed 18th November 2003.

Moskowitz, Robert, 'WLAN Testing Reports, "Debunking the Myth of SSID Hiding"', http://www.icsalabss.com/html/communities/WLAN/wp_ssid_hiding.pdf, report dated 1st December 2003, date accessed 26th January 2004.

NetMotion, 'Using NetMotion Mobility with WEP', http://www.netmotionwireless.com/support/technotes/2106.asp, article last reviewed on 13th August 2003, date accessed 20th November 2003.

NTA-Monitor, '"VPN Discovery and Fingerprinting Technique', http://www.nta-monitor.com/ike-scan/overview.htm, article undated, date accessed 12th November 2003.

NWFusion Encyclopedia, '802.11f',
http://www.nwfusion.com/links/Encyclopedia/0-
9/6043.html, date accessed 27th October 2003.

Parks, Gregory, '802.11e makes wireless universal',
http://www.nwfusion.com/news/tech/2001/0312tech.htm
l, article dated 3rd December 2001, date accessed 27th
October 2003.

PCQuest, 'WEP Security Cracked',
http://www.pcquest.com/content/topstories/wireless/103
081102.asp, article dated 11th August 2003, date
accessed, 7th November 2003.

Petty, Paul, and Brooks-Heath, Sooner, '802.11 Wireless
Security', PowerPoint presentation,
http://www.samos.aegean.gr/icsd/gkorm/wep.ppt, article
undated, accessed, 18th August 2003.

Phifer, Lisa, 'Better Than WEP', http://www.isp-
planet.com/fixed_wireless/technology/2002/better_than_
wep.html, article dated 1st February 2002, date accessed
23rd October 2003.

(PM) Phase Modulation,
http://whatis.techtarget.com/definition/0,,sid_gci213998,
00.html, accessed on 18th October 2003.

Poulsen, Kevin, 'War Driving by the Bay',
http://www.theregister.co.uk/content/archive/18285.html
, article dated 13th April 2003, accessed 23rd October
2003.

Proxim, Wireless Networks, 'Wireless Network Security',
http://www.proxim.com/learn/library/whitepapers/wireles
s_security.pdf, report undated, however copyright is
2003, date accessed 7th November 2003.

Robb, Drew, 'Sidebar: 802.11k – Management Standard
Ahead',
http://www.computerworld.com/mobiletopics/mobile/stor
y/0,10801,86131,00.html?f=x2, article date 20th October
2003, date accessed 23rd October 2003.

Roshan, Pejman, '802.1x authenticates 802.11 wireless', http://www.nwfusion.com/news/tech/2001/0924tech.htm l, article date 24th September 2001, date accessed 23rd October 2003.

Rysavy, Peter, 'Break Free with Wireless LANs', http://www.rysavy.com/Articles/BreakFree/BreakFree.ht m, article dated 29th October 2001, date accessed 29th October 2003.

Schoeneck, Rick, 'Wireless Honeypot', http://www.iirg.org/Richard_Schoeneck_GSEV.pdf, article dated 8th June 2003, dated accessed 21st November 2003.

SearchSecurity, 'IPSec', http://searchsecurity.techtarget.com/sDefinition/0,,sid14 _gci214037,00.html, article undated, date accessed 15th December 2003.

SearchSecurity.com Definitions, 'White Hat', http://searchSecurity.techtarget.com/sDefinition/0,,,sid14 _gci550882,00.html, article undated, date accessed, 4th December 2003.

Sikora, Axel, 'Wireless Personal and Local Area Networks', John Wiley & Sons Ltd, West Sussex, 2003.

Snyder, Joel, 'Down and Dirty with Wireless LAN Security', http://www.nwfusion.com/research/2002/0506ilabwlan.ht ml, article dated 5th June 2002, accessed on 20th August 2003.

Stone, Adam, 'The "Michael" Vulnerability', http://www.wi-fiplanet.com/columns/article.php/1556321, article dated 12th December 2002, date accessed 18th November 2003.

Sutherland, Ed, 'Stunning Visual Maps of Wireless LANs', http://www.wi-fiplanet.com/columns/article.php/999181, article dated 27th March 2002, date accessed 7th November 2003.

Sutherland, Ed, 'Examining Alternative to Patching WEP', http://www.wi-fiplanet.com/columns/article.php/958331, article dated 18th January 2002, date accessed 21st November 2003.

Sutton, Michael, 'Hacking the Invisible Network', iDefense, iAlert White Paper, http://www.rootshell.be/~doxical/download/docs/misc/Id efense_Hacking_the_invisible_network_(wireless).pdf, article dated 10th July 2002, accessed 18th August 2003.

SyDisTyKMoFo, 'Wireless Attacks Explained', http://www.astalavista.com/library/wlan/wlansecurity.ht m, article undated, accessed on 7th November 2003.

The 802.11 Report, 'This Week's Stories', e-mail newsletter, dated 21st January 2004. http://www.80211report.com

Thomas, Jeff, '802.11e brings QoS to WLANs', http://www.nwfusion.com/news/tech/2003/0623techupda te.html, article dated 23rd June 2003, date accessed 27th October 2003.

Tick, Drew, 'WPA for the SOHO Market: More Security means More Tech Support', http://www.itsecurity.com/papers/codered1.htm, article dated 13th June 2003, date accessed 15th December 2003.

Tourrilhes, Jean, 'Wireless Overview – The MAC Level', http://www.hpl.hp.com/personal/Jean_Tourrilhes/Linux/Li nux.Wireless.mac.html, last updated 3rd August 2000, accessed on 10th October 2003.

Tyrrell, Kevin, 'An Overview of Wireless Security Issues', http://www.giac.org/practical/GSCE/Kevin_Tyrrell_GSEC. pdf, article not dated, however copyright is 2003, article accessed 19th October 2003.

Ulanoff, Lance, 'Get free Wi-Fi, while its hot', http://www.pcmag.com/article2/0,4149,1195184,00.asp, article dated 16th July 2003, accessed 29th October 2003.

Vernier Networks, '"Wireless Security: protecting your 802.11 network', http://www.verniernetworks.com/wp.bitpipe.secur.protect .pdf, article dated September 2002, date accessed 20th November 2003.

Vines, Russell Dean, 'Wireless Security Essentials, Defending Mobile Systems from Data Piracy, Wiley Publishing Inc, 2002, Indiana, USA.

Walker, Jesse, 'Unsafe at any Key Size; An analysis of the WEP encapsulation', http://www.dis.org/wl/pdf/unsafe.pdf article dated 27th October 2000, date accessed 23rd October 2003.

Webopedia.com, SSID, http://www.webopedia.com/TERM/S/SSID.html, accessed on 31st October 2003.

Webopedia, 'Intrusion Detection System', http://networking.webopedia.com/TERM/I/Intrustion_det ection_system.html, article undated, date accessed 21st November 2003.

Whatis, 'Denial of Service', http://whatis.techtarget.com/definition/0,289893,sid0_gic 213591,00.html, last updated on 16th Nay 2001, date accessed 18th November 2003.

Whelan, Sean, 'Analysis of WEP and RC4 Algorithms', http://www.rootsecure.net/content/downloads/pdf_downl oads/wep_analysis.pdf, article dated March 2002, date accessed 19th October 2003.

Wi-Fi Alliance, 'Enterprise Solutions for WLAN security', http://www.wi-fi.org/OpenSection/pdf/Whitepaper_Wi_Fi_Entperise2-6-03.pdf , report dated 6th February 2003, date accessed 11th February 2004.

Wi-Fi Alliance, 'Wi-Fi Protected Access: Strong, standards-based, interoperable security for today's Wi-Fi networks', http://www.weca.net/OPenSection/pdf/Whitepaper_Wi-

Fi_Security4-29-03.pdf, article dated 29th April 2003, date accessed 18th November 2003.

Wi-Fi Planet Staff, '802.11 To Get Speed Boost?', http://wi-fiplanet.com/news/article.php/2184771, article dated 11th April 2003, accessed on 23rd October 2003.

Wi-FiPlanet, 'Minimising WLAN Security Threats', http://wi-fiplanet.com/tutorials/article.php/1457211, article dated 5th September 2002, date accessed 5th November 2003.

Wikipedia, 'Dictionary Attack', http://en.wikipedia.org/wiki/Dictionary_attack, article undated, date accessed 7th November 2003.

Wright, Joshua, 'Detecting Wireless LAN MAC Address Spoofing', http://home.jwu.edu/jwright/papers/wlan-mac-spoof.pdf, article dated 21st January 2003, date accessed 5th November 2003.

Wright, Joshua, 'Top 3 Attack Tools Threatening Wireless LANs',http://www.menet.umn.edu/~akash/links/sans_sec urity_webcast_wireless.pdf, article dated 3rd May 2003, date accessed 5th November 2003.